Some Years Of The Life Of The Duke And Duchess Of Marlborough

Sarah Jennings Churchill Marlborough

Some Years

OF THE

LIFE

OF

THE DUKE AND DUCHESS

OF

MARLBOROUGH,

FROM

THE FIRST COMING OF THE DUCHESS TO COURT,

TO

THE YEAR 1710.

Sarah (Jennings) Churchill Marlborough

Written by HERSELF.

London:

PRINTED BY AND FOR J. DAVIS, MILITARY CHRONICLE AND MILITARY
CLASSICS OFFICE, 14, CHARLOTTE-STREET, BLOOMSBURY, AND
TO BE HAD OF ALL THE BOOKSELLERS.—1817.

THE
ROYAL MILITARY CHRONICLE.

Supplement.]   NEW SERIES, JANUARY, 1817.   [Vol. VI.

Original Marlborough Papers.

SOME YEARS OF THE LIFE OF THE DUKE AND DUCHESS OF MARLBOROUGH,

BY THE DUCHESS HERSELF.

(In a recent Sale in Bond Street, the Original Marlborough Papers were sold at the enormous Price of Three Hundred Guineas. We have the satisfaction of laying before our Readers one of the most valuable of these,—Some Incidents of the Life of the Duke written by the Duchess herself, and therefore of undoubted authority.)

BEING now at the extreme point of life, and being very desirous of putting the life of my Lord Duke and myself in that point of view which will not injure our fair fame, I am induced to draw up this Narrative. It is as true as my memory of transactions long past will suffer me to make it.

I shall begin at the time, when, being a very young woman, the Princess Anne of Denmark first distinguished me. This was upon occasion of a quarrel with her sister Mary whilst King James was upon the throne. But I will go a little way further back.—My first acquaintance with the Princess began from our childhood. We used to play together in our infancy. This fondness (for such it was) grew with our years; and when she was married to the Prince of Denmark in 1683, it was by her own request that I was made one of the Ladies of her Bedchamber.

I was perhaps chiefly recommended to her by being somewhat more agreeable than the other persons about her. The first lady of the bedchamber was Lady Clarendon, a lady who looked like a mad-woman, and talked like a learned doctor. Indeed, never did I see a court so oddly composed. I owed my favour more to this than to my talent for flattery, to which I never submitted, and which our girlish love rendered unnecessary.

Kings and princes, for the most part, imagine they have a dignity peculiar to their birth and station, which ought to raise them above all connexion of friendship with an inferior. Their passion is to be admired and feared, to have subjects awfully obedient, and servants blindly obsequious to their pleasure. Friendship is an offensive word; it imports a kind of equality between the parties; it suggests nothing to the mind of crowns or thrones, high titles, or immense revenues, fountains of honour, or fountains of riches; prerogatives which the possessors would have always uppermost in the thoughts of those who are permitted to approach them.

The Princess had a different taste. A friend was what she most coveted. She grew uneasy to be treated by me with the form and ceremony due to her rank; nor could she bear from me the sound of words which implied in them distance and superiority. It was this turn of mind, which made her one day propose to me, that whenever I should happen to be absent from her, we might in all our letters write ourselves by feigned names, such as would import nothing of distinction of rank between us. Morley and Freeman were the names her fancy hit upon; and she left me to chuse by which of them I would be called. My frank open temper naturally led me to pitch upon Freeman, and so the Princess took the other; and from this time Mrs. Morley and Mrs. Freeman began to converse as equals, made so by affection and friendship.

Soon after the decease of King Charles the Second, Lord Clarendon was appointed Lord-Lieutenant of Ireland, to which country his Lady was to go with him. The Princess received a sensible joy from this event; not only as it released her from a person very disagreeable to her, but as it gave her an opportunity of promoting me to be first lady of her bed-chamber; which she immediately did.

During her father's whole reign she kept her court as private as she could, consistent with her station. What were the designs of that unhappy Prince every body knows. They came soon to shew themselves undisguised, and attempts were made to draw his daughter into them. The King indeed used no harshness with her; he only discovered his wishes, by putting into her hands some books and papers, which he hoped might induce her to a change of religion.

Lord Tyrconnel also, who had married my sister, took some pains with me, to engage me, if possible, to make use, for the same end, of that great favour which he knew I enjoyed with the Princess: but all his endeavours proved vain; and it was not long before all the danger blew over, the projects of that reign being effectually disappointed, almost as soon as they were openly avowed.

Upon the landing of the Prince of Orange in 1688, the King went down to Salisbury to his army, and the Prince of Denmark with him; but the news quickly came from thence, that the Prince of Denmark had left the King, and was gone over to the Prince of Orange, and that the King was coming back to London. This put the Princess into a great fright. She sent for me, told me her distress, and declared, *That rather than see her father she would jump out at window.* This was her very expression.

A little before, a note had been left with me, to inform me where I might find the Bishop of London (who in that critical time absconded), if her Royal Highness should have occasion for a friend. The Princess on this alarm, immediately sent me to the Bishop. I acquainted him with her resolution to leave the court, and to put herself under his care. It was hereupon agreed, that he should come about midnight in a hackney coach to the neighbourhood of the Cockpit, in order to convey the Princess to some place where she might be private and safe.

The Princess went to bed at the usual time to prevent suspicion. I came to her soon after; and by the back-stairs which went down from her closet, her Royal Highness, my Lady Fitzharding, and I, with one servant, walked to the coach, where we found the Bishop and the Earl of Dorset. They conducted us that night to the Bishop's house in the city, and the next day to my Lord Dorset's at Copt-hall. From thence we went to the Earl of Northampton's, and from thence to Nottingham, where the country gathered about the Princess; nor did she think herself safe, till she saw that she was surrounded by the Prince of Orange's friends.

The most remarkable thing that happened to the Princess during her stay at this place was a letter she received from Lord Clarendon. It was full of compliments, and at the same time full of complaints, that she had not told him of a thing he liked so well, that he might have had a share in it. *How well these compliments and the earnestness he shewed* (in a consulation held at Windsor, before the Prince of Orange came to London) *to have King James sent to the Tower*, agreed with his conduct afterwards, I shall leave to the world to judge.

Quickly after this, the King fled into France. The throne was hereupon declared vacant, and presently filled with the Prince and Princess of Orange. The Parliament thought proper to settle the crown on King William for life, and the Princess of Denmark gave her consent to it. The truth is, I persuaded her to consent to the project of that settlement, and to be easy under it, after it was made.

However, as I was fearful about every thing the Princess did, while she was thought to be advised by me, I could not satisfy my own mind, till I had consulted with several persons of undisputed wisdom and integrity, and particularly with the Lady Russel of Southampton-house, and Dr. Tillotson, afterwards Archbishop of Canterbury. I found them all unanimous in the opinion of the *expediency of the settlement proposed, as things were then situated.* In conclusion, therefore, I carried Dr. Tillotson to the Princess, and, upon what he said to her, she took care that no disturbance should be made by her pretended friends, the Jacobites who had pressed her earnestly to form an opposition.

It is certain, that the immediate occasion of the open breach between her Majesty and the Princess of Denmark was the Princess's refusing to obey the Queen's command *to remove me from about her person.* But no one, I think, can be so foolish as to imagine that the Queen's dislike of me was only on account of my being the wife of Lord Marlborough, who happened then to be in disgrace with the King; or that her Majesty would have insisted on a demand so painful to her sister, had they till then lived together in the harmony, which should naturally be preserved between sisters, especially when embarked in one common cause against a father in defence of religion.

To clear up this matter, then, and to discover the true sources of that famous quarrel, it will be necessary to recur to some preceding events which unfortunately led the way to it.

On the arrival of Queen Mary in England, the Princess of Denmark went to meet her, and there was great appearance of kindness between them. But this quickly 'wore off, and a visible coldness ensued; which I believe was partly occasioned by the persuasion the King had, that the Prince and Princess had been of more use to him, than they were ever like to be again, and partly by the different characters, and humours of the two sisters. It was indeed impossible they should be very agreeable companions to each other; because Queen Mary grew weary of any body who would not talk a great deal; and the Princess was so silent that she rarely spoke more than was necessary to answer a question. But this was not all. In the very beginning of that reign there happened some events, which, as they discovered an uncommon disregard in the Queen for her sister, must naturally produce an answerable discontent in the Princess. And here I cannot forbear saying, that whatever good qualities Queen Mary had to make her popular, it is too evident by many instances *that she wanted bowels.*

Of this she seemed to me to give an unquestionable proof the first day she came to Whitehall. I was one of those who had the honour to wait on her to her own apartment. She ran about it, looking into every closet and conveniency, and turning up the quilts upon the bed, as people do when they come into an inn, and with no other sort of concern in her appearance, but such as they express; a behaviour, which, though at that time I was extremely caressed by her, I thought very strange and unbecoming. For, whatever necessity there was of deposing King James, he was still her father, who had been so lately driven from that chamber, and that bed; and, if she felt no tenderness, I thought she should at least have looked grave, or even pensively sad, at so melancholy a reverse of his fortune.

The Princess, soon after the King's coming to Whitehall, had a mind to leave her lodgings (the way from which to the Queen's apartment was very inconvenient) and to go to those that had been the Duchess of Portsmouth's, which the King on her request told her she should have. But the Princess requesting also (for the conveniency of her servants) some other lodgings that lay nearer to those of the Duchess, this matter met with difficulty; though her Highness in exchange for what she asked was to give the whole Cockpit (which was more than an equivalent) to be disposed of for the King's use. For the Duke of Devonshire took into his head, that, could he have the Duchess of Portsmouth's lodgings, where there was a fine room for balls, it would give him a very magnificent air. And it was very plain, that, while this matter was in debate, between the King and Queen and Princess, my Lord Devonshire's chief business was to raise so many difficulties in making the Princess easy in those lodgings, as at last to gain his point. After many conversations upon the affair, the Queen told the Princess, " That she could not let her have the lodgings she desired for her servants, till my Lord Devonshire had resolved whether he would have them, or a part of the Cockpit:" Upon which the Princess answered, " She would then stay where she was, for she would not have my Lord Devonshire's leavings." So she took the Duchess of Portsmouth's apartment, granted her at first, and used it for her children, remaining herself at the Cockpit.

Much about the same time the Princess, who had a fondness for the house at Richmond (where she had lived when a child), and who, besides, thought the air of that place good for the children, desired that house of the Queen; but that likewise was refused her, though for many years no use had been made of it, but for Madame Possaire, a sister of my Lady Orkney, and Mr. Hill.

The Princess, notwithstanding these mortifications, continued to pay all imaginable respect to the King and Queen. But this did not hinder her Majesty from expressing a great deal of displeasure, when some steps were made in Parliament towards settling a revenue on the Prince and Princess. Taking her sister one night to task for it, she asked her, *What was the meaning of those proceedings?* To which the Princess answered, *She heard her friends had a mind to make her some settlement.* The Queen hastily replied with a very imperious air, *Pray what friends have you but the King and me?* I had not the honour to attend the Princess that night; but when she came back, she repeated this to me. And indeed I never saw her express so much resentment as she did at this usage; and I think it must be allowed she had great reason. For it was unjust in her sister not to allow her a decent provision, without an entire dependence on the King. And besides, the Princess had in a short time learnt that she must be very miserable, if she was to have no support but the friendship of the two persons her Majesty had mentioned.

After this the Queen said no more to the Princess on the subject of the settlement, though they met every day; and the affair went on so well in the House of Commons, that her friends were encouraged to propose for her a much larger revenue than was at last obtained; to prevent which, by gaining time, the King prorogued the Parliament.

The business however was resumed again at the next meeting; and then all possible endeavours were used, to engage me by flattery and by fear, to dissuade the Princess from the pursuit of a settlement. My Lady Fitzharding, who was more than any body in the Queen's favour, and for whom it was known that I had a singular affection, was the person chiefly employed in this undertaking. Sometimes she attacked me on the side of my own interest, telling me, "That if I would not put an end to measures so disagreeable to the King and Queen, it would certainly be the ruin of my Lord, and consequently of all our family." When she found that this had no effect, she endeavoured to alarm my fears for the Princess, by saying, " That those measures would in all probability ruin her: For no body, but such as flattered me, believed the Princess would carry her point; and in case she did not, the King would not think himself obliged to do any thing for her. That it was perfect madness in me to persist, and I had better ten thousand times persuade the Princess to let the thing fall, and so make all easy to the King and Queen."

But all this, and a great deal more that was said, was so far from inclining me to do what was desired of me, that it only made me more anxious about the success of the Princess's affair, and more earnest, if possible, in the prosecution of it. For, as I would have died, rather than have made my court to that reign by sacrificing the interest of the Princess; so there was nothing I dreaded more, than, by the least appearance of negligence, or coldness in the present cause, to give ground to suspect me of having been flattered into so base a conduct. I employed therefore all the powers I was capable of exerting to advance the design. I knew the thing was reasonable, the Princess's happiness was concerned in it, and there was a fair prospect of succeeding. Besides, that whatever happened in Parliament, the King could not well avoid giving some allowance to the next heir to the crown. And, if he should give her nothing, she had however, by the marriage-settlement, 20,000 l. a year, which would keep her in a retired way, much more agreeably than she could hope to live at court, if she depended on his generosity; of which I had no opinion: For the late Lord Godolphin had told me, that the King, on some meeting at the Treasury, speaking of the civil list, *wondered very much how the* Princess *could spend* 30,000l. *a year*, though it appeared afterwards that some of his favourites had more. And there were other parts of the King's conduct (which shall be mentioned in a proper place) whereby it sufficiently appeared, that I did not mistake in my opinion of his disposition.

But, to return to the affair in Parliament. A day or two before it was put to the vote in the House of Commons, I was extremely surprized by a message from the Duke of Shrewsbury, who, as he did not visit me, sent to desire to speak with me about business. When he came, he told me, "That he was sent by the King, who promised to give the Princess 50,000 l. a year, if she would desist from soliciting the settlement by Parliament, and that he was confident his Majesty would keep his word: That if he did not, he was sure he would not serve him an hour after he broke it." I said, that such a resolution might be very right as to his grace, but that I did not see it would be of any use to the Princess, if his Majesty should not perform the promise. The

Duke, to convince me of the reasonableness of what he proposed, added a great deal which had no effect; and I desired he would attend the Princess herself, to which he consented. I went to her at his request to acquaint her of his coming. Her answer to him was, "That she could not think herself in the wrong to desire a security for what was to support her; and that the business was now gone so far, that she thought it reasonable to see what her friends could do for her."

I need not tell you that the Princess carried her point, and that 50,000*l.* was settled by Parliament. For when the King found that he could not persuade her to an entire dependency upon him, he compounded the matter with her friends upon these terms, to hinder their insisting on a larger settlement. The Parliament had shewed an inclination that way: But it was at length thought advisable by the Princess's friends, that she should accept of 50,000*l.* securely settled, rather than have any farther struggle, considering the great power and influence of the crown, by means of its dependents.

Nevertheless, I was so fearful lest the Princess should suffer for want of good advice, that after I had heard of the Commons voting 50,000*l.* a year, I sent to speak with my Lord Rochester, and asked his opinion whether the Princess ought to be satisfied, or whether it was reasonable she should try to get more. (I did not then know how much his heart was bent on making his court to the Queen.) His answer to me was, "That he thought, not only that the Princess ought to be satisfied with 50,000 *l.* but that she ought to have taken it in any way the King and Queen pleased." Which made me reflect that he would not have liked that advice in the case of his own 4000*l.* a year from the Post-office settled on him and his son.

But I was not so uncivil, as to speak my thought, nor so foolish as to struggle any longer. For most of those who had been prevailed with to promote the settlement were tories, among whom my Lord Rochester was a very great man. Their zeal on the present occasion was, doubtless, to thwart King William; for I never observed that, on any other, they discovered much regard for the Princess of Denmark.

The success of the affair was chiefly imputed to the steadiness and diligence of my Lord Marlborough and me, both by those, to whom it was so exceedingly disagreeable, and by her, to whose happiness it was then so necessary.

On one side, it was the chief source of all the dissatisfaction of the King and Queen with us; and on the other, it was acknowledged by the Princess with as deep a sense of the kindness, as could be expressed, and in a manner generous to a very high degree.

A little above a year after the settlement was made, I was suprised with a letter from her, wherein she offered me the yearly pension of 1000*l.* Some of her words are these; "I have had something to say to you a great while, and I did not know how to go about it. I have designed, ever since my revenue was settled, to desire you would accept of a thousand pounds a year.———— I beg you would only look upon it as an earnest of my good-will, but never mention any thing of it to me; for I shall be ashamed to have any notice taken of such a thing from one that deserves more than I shall be ever able to return.

And some time afterwards, a little delay being made by her treasurer in the payment of it, she wrote another letter, wherein were these words; " 'Tis long since I mentioned this thing to dear Mrs. Freeman. She has all the reason in the world to believe I did not mean what I said, or that I have changed my mind, which are both so ill qualities, that I cannot bear you should have cause to think your faithful Morley is capable of being guilty of either."

The circumstances of my family at this time were not very great; yet I was so far from catching at so free and large an offer, that I could not persuade myself to accept of it, till I had sent the first letter to Lord Godolphin, and consulted him upon the matter. It was his opinion, that there was no reason in the world for me to refuse it. And perhaps no one else will think otherwise, who believes, as he did, that the settling of the Princess's revenue had been chiefly owing to my Lord Marlborough's indefatigable industry, and to mine.

The next difference that happened between the sisters, was upon the Prince's design of going to sea. He was carried to this resolution by his unwillingness to stay at home, while there was so much action abroad; and by the remembrance of the extreme ill usage he had met with, when, at a great expence, he attended his Majesty into Ireland. For the King would not suffer his Royal Highness to go in the coach with him: An affront never put upon a person of that rank before.

The Prince however submitted to this indignity, it being too late to take any measures to avoid it. Nor, during the whole campaign, did he fail in any part of duty or respect, though the King never took more notice of him, than if he had been a page of the back stairs.

You will allow, I believe, that it was very natural for the Prince to chuse a sea-expedition, rather than expose himself again to the like contemptuous usage. On his taking leave of the King, who was going to Flanders, he asked his Majesty's permission to serve him at sea as a volunteer, and without any command. The King said nothing; but immediately embraced him by way of adieu. Silence in such cases being generally taken for consent, the Prince prepared his equipage, and sent every thing on board. But the King, as it afterwards appeared, had left orders with the Queen, that she should neither suffer the Prince to go to sea, nor yet forbid him to go, if she could so contrive matters, as to make his staying at home his own choice.

The Queen observed the King's directions very exactly. She sent a great Lord to me, to desire I would persuade the Princess to keep the Prince from going to sea; and this I was to compass, without letting the Princess know that it was the Queen's desire. I answered, " That I had all the duty imaginable for the Queen, but that no consideration could make me so failing to my mistress, as I should think myself, if I spoke to her upon that occasion, and concealed the reason of it. That it was natural for the Princess to wish the Prince might stay at home, and be out of danger; but whether she could prevail in that matter, I did very much doubt. That nevertheless I would say to the Princess whatever her Majesty pleased, provided I might have the liberty to make use of her name." After this, the Queen sent my Lord Rochester to me, to desire much the same thing. " The Prince was not to go to sea, and his not-going was to appear his own choice." But after so much noise as had been made about his going, the Prince thought, that to send for his things back, without giving any reason for changing his design, would be making a very ridiculous figure, and therefore he would not submit. Upon which the Queen sent my Lord Nottingham in form, positively to forbid the Prince of Denmark's going to sea.

Notwithstanding all these things, the Queen and Princess lived, in appearance, for some time after, as if nothing had happened, till the King was pleased (without publicly assigning any particular reason) to remove my Lord Marlborough from all his employments. His Majesty sent Lord Nottingham to tell him, that he had no more occasion for his service. This event might, perhaps, be well enough accounted for, by saying, that Lord Portland had ever a great prejudice to my Lord Marlborough, and that my Lady Orkney (then Mrs. Villiers), though I had never done her any injury, except not making court to her, was my implacable enemy. But, I think, it is not to be doubted, that the principal cause of the King's message, was the court's dislike that any body should have so much interest with the Princess as I had, who would not implicitly obey every command of the King and Queen. The disgrace of my Lord Marlborough therefore was designed as a step towards removing me from about her.

A letter from the Queen to her sister, which I shall presently give you, affords ground for this opinion. And the behaviour of my Lord Rochester, who was much in the Queen's favour and councils, confirms it. He had warmly opposed my coming into the Princess's family, and he now shewed himself very desirous to have me removed, believing, without question, that could this be compassed, he should infallibly have the government of both sisters : though certainly, as to the Princess, he never discovered any such regard for her, as should give him a title to her confidence.

But to come to the sequel of the King's message. I solemnly protest, that the loss of my Lord Marlborough's employments would never have broke my rest one single night upon account of interest ; but, I confess, *the being turned out* is something very disagreeable to my temper. And, I believe it was three weeks, before my best friends could persuade me, that it was fit for me to go to a court, which (as I thought) had used my Lord Marlborough very ill.

However at last they prevailed. And I remembered the chief argument was urged by my Lord Godolphin, who said, that it could not be thought, I made any mean court to the King and Queen, since to attend the Princess, was only paying my duty where it was owing.

I waited therefore on my mistress to Kensington. The consequence was such, as my friends, having no reason to apprehend it, had never thought of. The next day the Queen wrote to her sister the following letter.

Kensington, Friday, the 5th of Feb.—" Having something to say to you, which I know will not be very pleasing, I chuse rather to write it first, being unwilling to surprise you ; though, I think, what I am going to tell you, should not, if you give yourself the time to think, that never any body was suffered to live at court in my Lord Marlborough's circumstances. I need not repeat the cause he has given the King to do what he has done, nor his unwillingness at all times to come to such extremities, though people do deserve it.

" I hope, you do me the justice to believe, it is as much against my will, that I now tell you, that, after this, it is very unfit Lady Marlborough should stay with you, since that gives her husband so just a pretence of being where he ought not.

" I think, I might have expected you should have spoke to me of it. And the King and I, both believing it, made us stay thus long. But seeing you was so far from it, that you brought Lady Marlborough hither last night, makes us resolve to put it off no longer, but tell you, she must not stay ; and that I have all the reason imaginable to look upon your bringing her, as the strangest thing that ever was done. Nor could all my kindness for you (which is ever ready to turn all you do the best way, at any other time) have hindered me shewing you that moment, but I considered your condition, and that made me master myself so far, as not to take notice of it then.

"But now I must tell you, it was very unkind in a sister, would have been very uncivil in an equal, and I need not say I have more claim. Which, though my kindness would make me never exact, yet when I see the use you would make of it, I must tell you, I know what is due to me, and expect to have it from you. 'Tis upon that account, I tell you plainly, Lady Marlborough must not continue with you in the circumstances her Lord is.

"I know this will be uneasy to you, and I am sorry for it; and it is very much so to me to say all this to you, for I have all the real kindness imaginable for you, and as I ever have, so will always do my part to live with you as sisters ought. That is, not only like so near relations, but like friends. And, as such, I did think to write to you. For I would have made myself believe your kindness for her made you at first forget that you should have for the King and Me; and resolved to put you in mind of it myself, neither of us being willing to come to harsher ways.

"But the sight of Lady Marlborongh having changed my thoughts, does naturally alter my style. And since by that I see how little you seem to consider what even in common civility you owe us, I have told you plainly; but withal asure you, that let me have never so much reason to take any thing ill of you, my kindness is so great, that I can pass over most things, and live with you, as becomes me. And I desire to do so merely from that motive. For I do love you, as my sister, and nothing but yourself can make me do otherwise. And that is the reason I chuse to write this, rather than tell it you, that you may overcome your first thoughts; and when you have well considered, you will find, that though the thing be hard, (which I again assure you I am sorry for) yet it is not unreasonable, but what has ever been practised, and what you yourself would do, were you in my place.

"I will end this with once more desiring you to consider the matter impartially, and take time for it. I do not desire an answer presently, because I would not have you give a rash one. I shall come to your drawing-room to-morrow before you play, because you know why I cannot make one: At some other time we shall reason the business calmly; which I will willingly do, or any thing else that may shew, it shall never be my fault if we do not live kindly together: Nor will I ever be other by choice, but your truly loving and affectionate sister,   "M. R."

I am perhaps to much concerned in the affair to be a proper judge of this letter. However I shall take the liberty to remark, that it seems not easy to reconcile the Queen's being sorry *to say so much*, with her employing at the same time such *useless repetitions;* as if it had been a pleasure to her to remind her sister of the distance between them, and of what was due from the Princess of Denmark to the Queen of England And I have wondered too, that so much kindness for a sister, then pregnant, and so much piety (for it must be observed the Queen was in devotion) did not hinder her from doing a thing which she owns is hard. Her Majesty indeed says, that "though it be hard, it is not unreasonable; but what has ever been practised, and what the Princess herself would do in her place." What the Princess would have done in her place, no body can tell: (she herself thought that she would not have done like the Queen.) But that it was not the *constant practice* is certain from many instances to the contrary, and particularly one, at that very time, in the case of the Marchioness of Halifax. And if the practice was not constant, how reasonable it was for the Queen to insist upon it in my case, I believe, I may safely leave to the judgment of her most zealous advocates.

For how disagreeable soever to the Queen my conduct had been, it would have proved no easy task to her, to find in any part of it a plausible reason for pressing the Princess to part with me. Would any person, who deserves to be in the *service* (not to say *intimate friendship*) of a Princess, have acted otherwise than I did, in relation to those points in which only I can be supposed to have disobliged their Majesties?

Would it have become me to be indifferent in the affair of the succession to the crown? and to be willing, *without the necessity of public good*, that my mistress, my friend, the Princess of Denmark, should yield her birthright to the Prince of Orange?

Could I, consistently with honour, have advised the Princess to desist from her attempt to get a maintenance settled by Parliament, and leave herself to the generosity of a King and Queen, who, by several slights and affronts put upon her, had shewed how very little they were concerned about her happiness?

Was the part which the Queen would have had me act, in relation to the Prince's going to sea, such, as any person, who had the least regard for his Highness's character and glory, would have consented to perform?

Doubtless my behaviour on all these occasions was criminal in the Queen's eyes; but this was only because she was Queen; for she had formerly looked upon my attachment and fidelity to her sister in a very different light.

As a proof of this, I shall here give two letters, which I received from her when she was Princess of Orange. I had many others in the same stile, which were lost in the hurry of the Revolution.

Loo, September 30th.—"Dr. Stanley's going to England is too good an opportunity for me to lose of assuring Lady Churchill, she cannot give me greater satisfaction than letting me know the firm resolution both Lord Churchill and you have taken, never to be wanting in what you owe your religion. Such a generous resolution I am sure must make you deserve the esteem of all good people, and my sister's in particular. I need say nothing of mine, you have it upon a double account, as my sister's friend, besides what I have said already; and you may be assured, that I shall always be glad of an occasion to shew it both to your Lord and you."

"I have nothing more to add; for your friendship makes my sister as dear to you as to me, I am persuaded we shall ever agree in our care for her; as, I belive, she and I should in our kindness for you, were we near enough to renew our acquaintance."   "MARIE."

"If it were as easy for me to write to my Lady Churchill as it is hard to find a safe hand, she might justly wonder at my long silence; but I hope she does me more justice than to think it my fault. I have little to say at present. To answer the melancholy reflections in your last is now too late; *but I hope my sister and you will never part.* I send you here one for her, and have not any more time now than only to assure you, that I shall never forget the kindness you shewed to her who is so dear to me. That, and all the good I have heard of you, will make me ever your affectionate friend, which I shall be ready to shew otherwise than by words whenever I have an opportunity."

It may be seen by these letters that the very same tenour of behaviour towards the Princess, which afterwards displeased the Queen, gave me at that time a recommendation to her affection; but the case was altered. And the Princess of Denmark was now, at the Queen of England's command, to put away *that kind dear friend* whom the Princess of Orange had *hoped she would never part with.* And she was to do this, not for any fault I had committed, but only because I was the wife of my Lord Marlborough, who happened to be in disgrace with the King.

Had the Queen really had custom on her side to countenance her in this harsh command, yet surely what was mere custom, and had no law to support it, might well have been neglected in the present case, in favour of reason and humanity.

She calls her command *hard,* because of the *kindness* she knew the Princess had for me. But had she mentioned the *reasons* too of that kindness, the severity of her injunction would have been more conspicuous. I speak not now of the Princess's inclination for me, previous to services on my part, but of that kindness which proceeded from her experience of my disinterested attachment to her interests and happiness. I say *disinterested* attachment. For the Princess knew that the Queen, after her coming into England, did me many honours which would have engaged some people to fix the foundation of their fortune in their favour; and that there was no person more likely than I, to rise high upon this bottom, if I could have been tempted to break the inviolable laws of friendship. Nor was there the least probability that the Princess should outlive the King and Queen, to recompense my fidelity, by such means as the royal prerogative furnishes. And as to the present power the Princess had to enrich me, her revenue was no such vast thing, as that I could propose to draw any mighty matters from thence; and, besides, Sir Benjamin Bathurst had the management of it, I had no share in that service.

I might add here, as a farther proof of the purity and integrity of my conduct, what I fancy will be easily believed : That on some occasions I could, without losing my mistress's affection, have sacrificed her cause, to make my court to the Queen. But so detestable a thought never entered into my soul : nor did I ever by asking any favour of the Queen, great or small, for my self or others, give her the least ground to hope, she could have any hold of me on the side of my interest.

Before the Princess returned an answer to the Queen's letter of command to dismiss me, she sent to my Lord Rochester, shewed him the answer she had prepared, and, with all the earnestness that can be imagined, desired he would use his interest to assist her, and that he would carry her letter; which last she could by no means persuade him to do. He told her he would speak to the Queen but could not give the letter to her. So the Princess sent it by one of her own servants. It contained these words.

"Your Majesty was in the right to think your letter would be very surprising to me. For you must needs be sensible enough of the kindness I have for my Lady Marlborough, to know, that a command from you to part with her must be the greatest mortification in the world to me ; and indeed of such a nature, as I might well have hoped your kindness to me would have always prevented. I am satisfied she cannot have been guilty of any fault to you. And it would be extremely to her advantage, if I could here repeat every word that ever she had said to me of you in her whole life. I confess, it is no small addtion to my trouble to find the want of your Majesty's kindness to me upon this occasion; since I am sure I have always endeavoured to deserve it by all the actions of my life.

"Your care of my present condition is extremely obliging. And if you would be pelased to add to it so far, as upon my account to recal your severe command (as I must beg leave to call it in a matter so tender to me, and so little reasonable' as I think, to be imposed upon me, that you would scarce require it from the meanest of your subjects) I should ever acknowledge it as a very agreeble mark of your kindness to me. And I must as freely own, that as I think this proceeding can be for no other intent than to give me a very sensible mortification, so there is no misery that I cannot readily resolve to suffer, rather than the thoughts of parting with her. If after all this that I have said, I must still find myself so unhappy as to be farther pressed in this matter, yet your Majesty may be assured that, as my past actions have given the greatest testimony of my respect both for the King and you, so it shall always be my endeavour, wherever I am, to preserve it carefully for the time to come, as becomes

"Your Majesty's very affectionate sister and servant,   "ANNE."
(From the Cockpit, Feb. 6th, 1692.)

To this the Princess received no answer but a message by my Lord Chamberlain *to forbid my continuing any longer at the* Cockpit.

It was the opinion of several people, that the King had no more power to remove any body out of that house, than out of any other buildings on that side the park, it having been bought of the Duke of Leeds, and settled at the Princess's marriage in King Charles's time on her, and her heirs. But the Princess had resolved to do every thing respectful to the King and Queen, except yielding in that single point of parting with me. And therefore instead of insisting on the right, which she had in common with every other subject, *of being mistress in her own house,* she wrote to the Queen the following letter.

"I am sorry to find that all I have said myself, and my Lord Rochester for me, has not effect enough to keep your Majesty from persisting in a resolution, which you are satisfied must be so great a mortification to me, as, to avoid it, I shall be obliged to retire, and deprive myself of the satisfaction of living where I might have frequently opportunities of assuring you of that duty and respect, which I always have been, and shall be desirous to pay upon all occasions.

"My only consolation in this extremity is, that not having done any thing in all my my life, to deserve your unkindness, I hope I shall not be long under the necessity of absenting myself from you; the thought of which is so uneasy to me, that I find myself too much indisposed to give your Majesty any farther trouble at this time."   *(February 8th, 1692.)*

Though my Lord Rochester be mentioned in this letter, as having employed his good offices to prevail with the Queen to change her determination, there is little reason to think that his intercession could be very warm or urgent after the refusal he made to carry the former letter, though pressed to it by the most earnest entreaties.

At the same time, that the Princess resolved to leave the Cockpit, she sent to speak with the Duchess of Somerset, of whom she desired to borrow Sion for some little time. The Duchess made her many expressions, and very soon after, having spoke to the Duke of Somerset of it, waited on her again, to acquaint her, in a very respectful manner, that Sion was at her service.

As soon as this was known, the King did all he could to dissuade the Duke from letting the Princess have the house; but his Grace had too much greatness of mind to go back from his promise; so there was an end of the matter.

Before the Princess removed from the Cockpit, she waited upon her Majesty at Kensington, making all the professions that could be imagined, to which the Queen was as insensible as a statue. When she did answer her it was in the stile of her letter.

Soon after the Princess's going to Sion, a dreadful plot broke out, which was said to have been hid somewhere, I don't know where, in a flower-pot; and my Lord Marlborough was sent to the Tower.

To commit a peer to prison it was necessary there should be an affidavit from some body of the treason. My Lord Romney therefore, secretary of state, had sent to one Young, who was then in jail for perjury and forgery, and paid his fine, in order to make him what they call a *legal evidence.* For as the court-lawyers said, Young not having lost his ears, was an *irreproachable witness.* I shall not dwell on the story of this fellow's villainy, the Bishop of Rochester having given a full Account of it in print.

Whether my Lord Marlborough's conspiracy with this Young was what the Queen meant in her letter to the Princess, where she speaks "of the cause my Lord Marlborough had given the King to do what he had done, and of his unwillingness to come to such extremities, though people did deserve it," I know not. Nor indeed could I ever learn what cause the King assigned for his displeasure. But it is natural to think he would give the best reason he could for using in that manner a man, who had done so much for the Revolution. Every one knows, that my Lord Marlborough had considerable employments under King James, and might have hoped to be as great a favourite as any body, could he have assisted in bringing about that unhappy Prince's scheme of fixing Popery and Arbitrary Power in England. It was highly improbable therefore, that he, who had done so much, and sacrificed so much for the preservation of the religion and liberty of his country, should on a sudden engage in a conspiracy to destroy them. And though these considerations had no weight with the King, they had so much with my Lord Devonshire, my Lord Bradford, and the late Duke of Montagu, that they thought it infamous to send my Lord Marlborough to prison upon such evidence; and therefore when the warrant for his committment came to be signed at the council-table, they refused to put their hands to it, though at that time they had no particular friendship for him. My Lord Bradford's behaviour was very remarkable; for he made my Lord Marlborough a visit in the Tower, while some of our friends, who had lived in our family like near relations for many years, were so fearful of doing themselves hurt at court, that in the whole time of his confinement, they never made him or me a visit, nor sent to enquire how we did, for fear it should be known.

My Lord Marlborough's being sent to the Tower having obliged me to go and stay at London to attend the affair of his releasement, I there received, among many others, in the same stile of tenderness, the following letters from the Princess. I have transcribed these, to shew you her goodness to me upon all occasions, and to give you a more lively impression of the cruelty of the Queen's command, that enjoined her sister to part with a friend so dear to her heart, merely to gratify the royal pride in a point of ceremony.

To Lady Marlborough.—"Though I have nothing to say to my dear Mrs. Freeman, I cannot help enquiring how she and her Lord does. If it be not convenient to you to write, when you receive this, either keep the bearer till it is, or let me have a word or two from you by the next opportunity when it is easy to you at any time, much less now, when you have so many things to do, and think of. All I desire to hear from you at such a time as this, is, that you and your's are well. Which, next to having my Lord Marlborough out of his enemies' power, is the best news that can come to her, who, to the last moment of her life, will be dear Mrs. Freeman's."

" *Friday Night.*"

To Lady Marlborough.—"I give dear Mrs. Freeman a thousand thanks for her kind letter, which gives me an account of her concerns; and that is what I desire more to know than any other news. I shall reckon the days and hours, and think the time very long till the term is out, for both your sake and my Lord Marlborough's, that he may be at liberty, and your mind at ease. You do not say any thing of your health, which makes me hope you are well, at least, not worse than when you were here. And, dear Mrs. Freeman don't say when I can see you, if I come to town; therefore I ask what day will be most convenient to you? For, though all days are alike to me, I should be glad you would name one, because I am to take some physick, and would order that accordingly. I confess, I long to see you, but am not so unreasonable to desire that satisfaction till it is easy to you. I wish with all my soul, that you may not be a true prophetess, and that it may be soon in our power to enjoy one another's company, more than it has been of late; which is all I covet in this world."

To Lady Marlborough.—"I am sorry with all my heart, dear Mrs. Freeman meets with so many delays; but it is a comfort, they cannot keep Lord Marlborough in the Tower longer than the end of the term; and, I hope, when the Parliament sits, care will be taken that people may not be clapt up for nothing, or else there will be no living in quiet for any body, but insolent Dutch, and sneaking mercenary Englishmen. Dear Mrs. Freeman, farewel; be assured your faithful Mrs. Morley can never change; and, I hope, you do not in the least doubt of her kindness, which, if it be possible, encreases every day, and that can never have an end but with her life. Mrs. Morley hopes her dear Mrs. Freeman will let her have the satisfaction of hearing from her again to-morrow." *(Thursday.)*

To Lady Marlborough.—"Dear Mrs. Freeman may easily imagine, I cannot have much to say, since I saw her. However, I must write two words. For though I believe she does not doubt of my constancy, seeing how base and false all the world is, I am of that temper, I think, I can never say enough to assure you of it. Therefore give me leave to assure you they can never change me. And there is no misery I cannot readily resolve to suffer, rather than the thought of parting from you. And I do swear, I would sooner be torn in pieces, than alter this my resolution. My dear Mrs. Freeman, I long to hear from you."

To Lady Marlborough.—"My dear Mrs. Freeman was in so dismal a way when she went from hence, that I cannot forbear asking, how she does, and if she has yet any hopes of Lord Marlborough's being soon at liberty. For God's sake, have a care of your dear self, and give as little way to melancholy thoughts as you can. If I could be as often with you as those that have it in their power, but not in their will, you should seldom be alone, but though I have not that satisfaction, as much as I desire, I assure you, my heart is always with you; and if wishes signified any thing, you would have no uneasy minute.

"Though I long of all things to hear from my dear Mrs. Freeman, I am not so unreasonable as to expect the groom should come back to-night, if he comes to you at an unreasonable hour; therefore keep him till it is easy to you to write. But I am in hopes, I shall have a word or two before I go to bed; because my dear Mrs. Freeman has promised I shall hear from you.

"I fancy ass's milk would do you good, and that is what you might take morning or afternoon, as it is most convenient.

"I had no sooner sealed my letter, but I received my dear Mrs. Freeman's, for which I gave her a thousand thanks, and am overjoyed at the good news you send me, which I hope will cure you of every thing."

To Lady Marlborough.—"I am in pain to know how my dear Mrs. Freeman does, for she is not used to complain, nor to be let blood for a little thing; and therefore I cannot help enquiring what is the matter, and how she finds herself now? I can come either to London or Camden-house to-morrow or Monday, or any other day. If you will let me know where and when, and what time I may have the satisfaction of seeing you, your faithful Morley will be sure to meet you."

Your Lordship sees by these letters of tenderness how impossible it must have been for the Princess to comply with the Queen's desire, had it appeared less unreasonable than it did. However, she was very attentive not to be wanting in any point of *due* respect. Falling in labour at Sion, she sent Sir Benjamin Bathurst to present her humble duty to the Queen, and acquaint her with it, and that she was much worse than she used to be; as she really was. The Queen did not think fit to see the messenger, nor to make any answer.

Notwithstanding this, when the Princess was brought to bed of a child, that died some minutes after the birth, she sent my Lady Charlotte Beverwaert to inform her Majesty of what had happened. My Lady waited some considerable time before the Queen saw her. The reason of this was my Lord Rochester's not being present, when the message came. After some conversation with him, the Queen sent for my Lady Charlotte, and told her, she would go that afternoon and see the Princess at Sion, and she was there very soon after the notice arrived.

She came attended by the Ladies Derby and Scarborough. I am sure it will be necessary to have a good voucher to persuade your Lordship of the truth of what I am going to relate. The Princess herself told me, that the Queen never asked her how she did, nor expressed the least concern for her condition, nor so much as took her by the hand. The salutation was this: "I have made the first step, by coming to you, and I now expect you should make the next by removing Lady Marlborough." The Princess answered, "That she had never in all her life disobeyed her, except in that one particular, which she hoped would, some time or other, appear as unreasonable to her Majesty, as it did to her." Upon which the Queen rose up and went away, repeating to the Prince, as he led her to the coach, the same thing she had said to the Princess.

My Lady Derby did not come to the bed-side, nor make the least enquiry after her health, though the Princess had recommended her, for Groom of the Stole, to the Queen, on her accession to the crown. Lady Scarborough indeed behaved herself as became her on that occasion, and afterwards asked the Queen's leave to visit me, because we had been old acquaintance: which was granted.

I have heard that the Queen, when she came home, was pleased to say, "she was sorry she had spoke to the Princess; who, she confessed, had so much concern upon her at renewing the affair, that she trembled and looked as white as the sheets. But if her Majesty was really touched with compassion, it is plain, by what followed, that she overcame herself extremely. For presently after this visit, all company was forbid waiting on the Princess; and her guards were taken away.

I do not see how the most zealous advocates for the Queen can vindicate her in these proceedings to au only sister, nor how a man of that mighty under-standing, my Lord Rochester was said to have, could think, that a visit (which the Queen made to every countess) was so extraordinary a grace to a sister, that it should oblige her to do, what she had retired from the court to avoid.

I must observe to your Lordship, that the King was not in England, when this last thing happened. My Lord Rochester was the Queen's oracle; and whether he had any share or not in beginning the ill usage of the Princess, he was without question the prosecutor of it.

I fancy, you have been wishing, during all this story, that I had made some proposal to the Princess, to free her from the trouble she was in, and to save her from such indignities, as surely have seldom, if ever, been offered to the presumptive heir of a crown. When you have read some letters I had from her on the occasion, I believe you will be satisfied I did my part. I assure you, that from the very beginning of the difference, it was my earnest request to her to let me go from her; for though, had I been in her place, I would not have complied with the Queen's demand, yet I thought that in mine, I could not discharge what I owed to the Princess, without employing every argument my thoughts could suggest, to prevail with her to part with me. But whenever I said any thing that looked that way, she fell into the greatest passion of tender-ness and weeping that is possible to imagine. And though my situation, at that time, was so disagreeble to my temper, that, could I have known how long it was to last, I could have chose to go to the Indies sooner, than to endure it; yet, had I been to suffer a thousand deaths, I think I ought to have submitted rather than have gone from her against her will.

As soon as the Princess was recovered from a fever, which followed the in-disposition of her lying-in, (and which, I believe, was in great measure caused by her trouble) she began to think she should be found fault with, if she did not express her thankfulness for the great honour the Queen had done her. Whereupon she sent to Doctor Stillingfleet, Bishop of Worcester, to come to see her, intending to write to the Queen by him, and to make use of his credit to soften her. On this occasion, I had from her the two following letters.

To Lady Marlborough—"I had last night a very civil answer from the Bis-hop of Worcester, whom I sent to speak with, but have heard nothing more of him since, so I dare not venture to go to London to-day, for fear of missing him. If he comes in any time to-morrow, I will not fail of being with my dear Mrs. Freeman, about five or six o'clock, unless you are to go to the Tower. And if you do, pray be so kind as to let me know time enough to stop my jour-ney. For I would not go to London, and miss the satisfaction of seeing you. I could not forbear writing though I had nothing more to say, but that it is impossible ever to express the kindness I have for dear Mrs. Freeman."

To Lady Marlborough.—"Sir Benjamin telling me you were not come to town at three o'clock, makes me in pain to know how your son does, and I can't help enquiring after him and dear Mrs. Freeman. The Bishop of Worces-ter was with me this morning before I was dressed. I give him my letter to the Queen, and he has promised to second it, and seemed to undertake it very willingly: Though by all the discourse I had with him, (of which I will give you a particular account when I see you) I find him very partial to her. The last time he was here, I told him you had several times desired you might go from me, and I have repeated the same thing again to him. For you may easily imagine, I would not neglect doing you right upon all occasions. But I beg it again for Christ Jesus's sake, that you would never name it any more to me. For be assured, if you should ever do so cruel a thing as to leave me, from that moment I shall never enjoy one quiet hour. And should you do it without asking my consent (which if I ever give you, many I never see the face of heaven) I will shut myself up, and never see the world more, but live where I may be forgotten by human kind.

The letter which the Princess sent to the Queen by the Bishop of Worcester was in these terms.

Sion, the 20th of May.—"I have now, God be thanked, recovered my strength well enough to go abroad. And though my duty and inclination would both lead me to wait upon your Majesty, as soon as I am able to do it, yet I have of late had the misfortune of being so much under your Majesty's displeasure, as to apprehend, there may be hard constructions made upon any thing I either do, or not do, with the most respectful intentions. And I am in doubt whether the same arguments, that have prevailed with your Majesty to forbid people from shewing their usual respects to me, may not be carried so much farther, as not to permit me to pay my duty to you. That, I acknowledge, would be a great increase of affliction to me? and nothing but your Majesty's own command shall ever willingly make me submit to it. For whatever reason I may think in my own mind I have to complain of being hardly used, yet I will strive to hide it, as much as possible. And though I will not pretend to live at the Cockpit, unless you would be so kind as to make it easy to me, yet wherever I am, I will endeavour always to give the constant marks of duty and respect, which I have in my heart for your Majesty, as becomes.

"Your Majesty's very affectionate sister and servant,   " ANNE."

To this the Queen returned the following answer.

To the Princess.—"I have received your's by the Bishop of Worcester, and have very little to say to it: since you cannot but know, that as I never used compliments, so now they will not serve,

" 'Tis none of my fault, we live at this distance, and I have endeavoured to shew my willingness to do otherwise. And I will do no more. Don't give yourself any unnecessary trouble: for be assured it is not words can make us live together as we ought. You know what I required of you. And I now tell you if you doubted it before, that I cannot change my mind, but expect to be complied with, or you must not wonder if I doubt of your kindness. You can give me no other marks, that will satisfy me. Nor can I put any other construction upon your actions than what all the world must do, that sees them. These things don't hinder me being very glad to hear you are so well, and wishing you may continue so, that you may yet, while 'tis in your power, oblige me to be your affectionate sister.   " MARIE R."

What sentiments the Princess had on receiving this harsh, peremptory declaration from the Queen, you will see by her letter to me on that occasion.

The Princess to Lady Marlborough.—" I am very sensibly touched with the misfortune that my dear Mrs. Freeman has had of losing her son, knowing very well, what it is to lose a child: but she knowing my heart so well, and how great a share I bear in her concerns, I will not say any more on this subject, for fear of renewing her passion too much.

" Being now at liberty to go where I please, by the Queen's refusing to see me, I am mightily inclined to go to-morrow, after dinner, to the Cockpit, and from thence privately in a chair to see you, some time next week. I believe it will be time for me to go to London to make an end of that business of Berkeley house.

" The Bishop brought me the Queen's letter early this morning, and by that little he said, he did not seem so well satisfied with her, as he was yesterday. He has promised to bear me witness, that I have made all the advances, that were reasonable. And I confess, I think, the more it is told about, that I would have waited on the Queen, but that she refused seeing me, is the better : and therefore I will not scruple saying it to any body, when it comes in my way.

" There were some in the family, as soon as the news came this morning of our fleet's beating the French, that advised the Prince to go in the afternoon to compliment the Queen. And another asked me, if I would not send her one ? but we neither of us thought there was any necessity of it then, and much less since I received this arbitrary letter. I don't send you the original for fear any accident may happen to the bearer : for I love to keep such letters by me for my own justification. Sure never any body was used so by a sister ! but I thank God I have nothing to reproach myself withal in this business, but the more I think of all that has passed, the better I am satisfied. And if I had done otherwie, I should have deserved to have been the scorn of the world, and to be trampled upon as much as my enemies would have me.

" Dear Mrs. Freeman, farewel. I hope in Christ you will never think more of leaving me, for I would be sacrificed to do you the least service, and nothing but death can ever make me part with you. For if it be possible I am every day more and more yours.

" I hope your Lord is well. It was Mr. Maul and Lady Fitzharding that advised the Prince and me to make our compliments to the Queen."

. As your Lordship has here read the Princess's final resolution, you may now perhaps be curious to know, what were the Prince of Denmark's dispositions, in relation to this affair. Some parts of the following letters will satisfy you in *this point*, as the rest will confirm what has been said of my desiring to leave the Princess ; the ill treatment she met with, in this reign, from the beginning ; and the obligations she thought herself under to Lord Marlborough and me for our fidelity and diligent services to her.

To Lady Marlborough.—" I really long to know how my dear Mrs. Freeman got home ; and now I have this opportunity of writing, she must give me leave to tell her, if she should ever be so cruel to leave her faithful Mrs. Morley, she will rob her of all the joy and quiet of her life ; for if that day should come, I could never enjoy a happy minute, and I swear to you I would shut myself up and never see a creature. You may easily see all this would have come upon me, if you had not been. If you do but remember what the Q. said to me the night before your Lord was turned out of all ; then she begun to pick quarrels ; and if they should take off twenty or thirty thousand pound, have I not lived upon as little before ? When I was first married we had but twenty (it is true indeed the King was so kind to pay my debts) and if it should come to that again, what retrenchment is there, in my family, I would not willingly make, and be glad of that pretence to do it : never fancy, dear Mrs. Freeman, if what you fear should happen, that you are the occasion ; no, I am very well satisfied, *and so is the Prince too*, it would have been so however, for   is capable of doing nothing but injustice ; therefore rest satisfied, you are no ways the cause ; and let me beg once more, for God's sake, that you would never mention parting more, no nor so much as think of it ; and if you should ever leave me, be assured it would break your faithful Mrs. Morley's heart." *(Friday Morning.)*

" I hope my dear Mrs. Freeman will come as soon as she can, this afternoon, that we may have as much time together as we can ; I doubt you will think me very unreasonable for saying this, but I really long now to see you again, as much as if I had not been so happy this month.

To Lady Marlborough.—" In obedience to dear Mrs. Freeman, 'I have told the Prince all she desired me, and he is so far from being of another opinion, if there had been occasion he would have strengthened me in my resolutions, and we both beg you would never mention so cruel a thing any more.' Can you think either of us so wretched that for the sake of twenty thousand pound, and to be tormented from morning to night with flattering knaves and fools, we should forsake those, we have such obligations to, and that we are the occasion of all their misfortunes ? Besides, can you believe we will truckle to   who from the first moment of his coming has used us at that rate, as we are sensible he has done, and that all the world can witness, that will not let their interest weigh more with them, than their reason. But suppose I did submit, and that the King could change his nature so much, as to use me with humanity, how would all reasonable people dispise me ? How would laugh at me and please himself with having got the better? And which is much more, how would my conscience reproach me for having sacrificed it, my honour, reputation, and all the substantial comforts of this life for transitory interest, which, even to those who make it their idol, can never afford any real satisfaction, much less to a virtuous mind : No, my dear Mrs. Freeman, never believe your faithful Mrs. Morley will ever submit. She can wait with patience for a sun-shine day, and if she does not live to see it, yet she hopes England will flourish again. Once more give me leave to beg you would be so kind never to speak of parting more, for let what will happen, that is the only thing can make me miserable." *(Tuesday Morning.)*

His Royal Highness continued steady in his opinion to the last, notwithstanding that almost all the servants in the family, and especially those whom I had brought into it, were frequently pressing him to have me removed. My Lord Berkeley indeed, though I believe he did not know, that he was obliged to me for his employment of Groom of the Stole, said some thing very handsome to the Prince, (as the Princess told me) to strengthen him in the contrary resolution. But my Lord Lexington, who was not so ignorant of the service I had done him, made the first return for it, by speaking to the Prince *to put her out, who had put him in.*

But of all that happened to me of this kind, nothing surprised so much, as the behaviour of Mr. Maul. I had not only brought him to be bed-chamber man to the Prince, when he was quite a stranger to that court, but, to mend his salary, had invented an employment for him, that of overlooking the Princess's accounts: And I had done this without having been asked to do it. I had indeed a great value for him, and thought him so worthy a man, and so much my friend, that I might safely have trusted to his care my most important concerns. But you will see how extremely I was mistaken. This man never came near me, during that time of trouble. And when I chanced to meet him at Sion, avoided as much as he could, even to make me a bow ; apprehending, I believe, that I should ask him to be Lord Marlborough's bail : Not that I then guessed this to be the reason ; but I thought so afterwards ; because, notwithstanding his strange coldness. even to rudeness, as soon as it was known that Lord Shrewsbury, Lord Burlington, Lord Carbury, and Lord Halifax were to be bail for my Lord Marlborough he came to see me, and offered himself for that service, making as if he knew nothing of what was so public. I thanked him, and told him, Lord Marlborough had friends, who would bail him, but that one of his best friends, was a paper that lay upon the table, which I had often kissed, *The Act of Habeas Corpus.*

But this was not the greatest proof I had of Mr. Maul's ingratitude. He was one of those, who were most urgent with the Prince, that he would prevail with the Princess to put me away. For this end he took more pains than ordinary in attending on him. And I cannot help telling a very foolish thing he said to his Royal Highness, and what one would not have expected from a man that kept good company. The Prince one day, after being much pressed by him, on my subject, answered, "That he had so much tenderness for the Princess, that he could not desire to make her so uneasy, as he knew the parting with me would do. And besides, he had done a great deal, and had been very ill used." To which Mr. Maul replied, "That it was true his Highness had done a great deal; but if he refused this thing, it was like a cow, that gave a great deal of milk, and then kicked it down."

Very soon after this eloquent, but unsuccessful pleading of Mr. Maul (who had certainly been employed by my Lord Rochester) a letter came to the Princess, from his Lordship, on occasion of the Queen's having forbid people to go to her.

The contents of it were these.

"Madam,—I am afraid, I may be guilty of too great presumption in giving your Royal Highness the trouble of a letter; but I do it with so good intentions, that I hope you cannot be angry with me for it. And now that one is unhappily restrained from the honour of waiting upon your Royal Highness, there is no other way but this to make an offer of my humble duty to you. It is a very uncomfortable reflection for me to make, but being so really concerned, as I am sure I am, for your Royal Highness's happiness, I should be so unfortunate as to be wholly useless to you, at a time, when your Royal Highness cannot but think yourself, that you have the use of every body, that are truly and faithfully your servants. And however I have been so mistaken in my judgment, as to have never offered any thing to your Royal Highness, worth your approbation, I do, with all humility, submit my poor opinion to that of your Royal Highness; but beg you to believe, it is not flattery to any body else, nor any other consideration that has made me be of the mind I was; but only the want of a better understanding, to be able to think of something more for your service. And being thus incapable of myself to propose any thing that is agreeable to you, I take this occasion humbly to offer to your Royal Highness all the little service you may judge me fit to be employed in, and most earnestly to beseech you to believe, that if I can be of any use in the world to your Royal Highness, there is nothing that I would endeavour with greater satisfaction to myself, than at this time to express the great concern, I presume to say I have, for your Royal Highness, by any thing that I can do for your service. And if any thing I have taken the confidence to say be worth your taking notice of, the least signification of your pleasure will bring me at all times to receive the honour of any of your commands; and the duty and zeal and passion, I have for your true interest and prosperity, will, I hope, make some amends for the want of a better judgment and capacity, which I acknowledge every body has a greater share of than,

" Madam, Your Royal Highness's most obedient and most dutiful servant,
" ROCHESTER."

I cannot help thinking, that there is something very absurd in the *affected modesty* and *profound respectfulness* of this letter; where his Lordship owns, that every body has more judgment and capacity than he, and with all humility, submits his poor opinion to that of her Royal Highness, and at that same time, lets her know that this *poor opinion* which he so *submits*, shall entirely *govern* him in his behaviour towards her. And the perfect self approbation he discovers after lamenting the mistake of his judgment, is no less ridiculous. For he plainly intimates some expectation, that she will send for him again, and confess the wisdom of the senseless advice he had given her. I make no scruple to call his Lordship's advice *senseless*. For how unworthy soever he might think me of the extraordinary affection the Princess had for me, he could not hope (unless he were really the simpleton he says he is) that what had latley happened would be a means to cure her of it in any degree: and he must know, that while she retained that affection, she could not part with me, without *extreme unhappiness* to herself. And what had he to propose, as a compensation to her for this unhappiness? Not the *inward satisfaction* nor the *outward glory* of having obeyed any law of God or of the land, by removing me from her; but only the *empty* advantage of putting an end to their Majesties' *open* displeasure with her; a displeasure, which did her no real hurt, and which, being so occasioned as it was, gained her credit with every mortal that had a heart.

The Princess was not imposed upon by his Lordship's *duty* or *zeal* or *passion* for her prosperity. She sent him the following answer to his letter.

To the Earl of Rochester.—" I gave you many thanks for the compliments and expressions of service which you make me, in your letter: which I should be much better pleased with than I am, if I had any reason to think them sincere."

" It is a great mortification to me, to find, that I still continue under the misfortune of the Queen's displeasure. I had hopes, in time, the occasion of it would have appeared as little reasonable to the Queen, as it has always done to me. And if you would have persuaded me of the sincerity of your intentions, as you seem to desire, you must give me leave to say, I cannot think it very hard for you to convince me of it, by the effects. And till then I must beg leave to be excused, if I am apt to think, this great mortification, which has been given me, cannot have proceeded from the Queen's own temper, who, I am persuaded, is both more just in herself, than that comes to, as well as more kind to

" Your very affectionate friend,   " ANNE."

And now the business of his Lordship was to make the Queen's order be complied with. He took great pains in it himself; and all the ladies of the bedcamber were employed either to speak or write to their relations and acquaintance. And this matter was so well followed, that, at last, the Queen herself sent to my Lady Grace Pierpoint, " to desire that she would not go to the Princess;" adding, " that if she did, she should not come to her, for she would see no body that went to her sister." My Lady Grace's answer was, "That she thought she owed a respect to the Princess; that she had been civilly treated by her; and that if her Majesty would not allow her to pay her duty to her, she would go no more to the Queen, and the oftner to the Princess."

But this generous example of refusing meanly to submit to an unreasonable order, was followed by very few, except those whom my Lord Marlborough and I engaged to pay the Princess all the respect possible. Two or three jacobite ladies also came to her, because (as it was easy to observe) all of that interest rejoiced much at the quarrel.

My Lady Thanet was one of the first, who, like my Lord Rochester (and I conclude, not without his advice) made her excuse to the Princess by letter. I cannot now find it; but you may guess at the contents of it by the Princess's answer, which was this.

To the Dowager Countess of Thanet.—" It is no small addition to my unhappiness in the Queen's displeasure, that I am deprived, by it, of the satisfaction of seeing my friends; especially of such as seem desirous to see me, and to find by those late commands, which her Majesty has given you, that her unkindness to me is to have no end. The only comfort I have in these great hardships, is, to think, how little I have deserved them from the Queen. And that thought, I hope, will help me to support them with less impatience.

"I am the less surprised at the strictness of the Queen's command to you, upon this occasion, since I have found she can be so very unkind to &c."

It was almost a year after this, and when it was of very little use, before Lady Thanet first, and then Lady Hyde, came to wait on the Princess. And their visits afterwards were very rare, and only upon extraordinary occasions, as a lying-in, or some great illness.

I have already mentioned, besides this prohibition to visit the Princess, the taking away of her guards. And these were not the only methods devised to mortify her. One very ridiculous thing was done with this view, while the Princess was at Bath. The following letter, signed by the Earl of Nottingham, Secretary of State, was dispatched to the Mayor of the town, a tallow-chandler.

"SIR,—The Queen has been informed, that yourself and your brethren have attended the Princess with the same respect and ceremony, as have been paid to the Royal Family, perhaps you may not have heard what occasion her Majesty has had to be displeased with the Princess. And therefore I am commanded to acquaint you, that your are not for the future to pay her Highness any such respect or ceremony, without leave from her Majesty, who does not doubt of receiving from you and your brethren, this public mark of your duty.

"I am your most humble servant, "NOTTINGHAM."

The King being abroad when this letter was writ, and the Queen being at that time wholly in my Lord Rochester's hands, every body concluded, that it was done by his advice. And I am myself the more fully persuaded of it, from the fondness he discovered for such sort of pageantry, when (in the beginning of Queen Anne's reign) he made his progress, in those parts, and took pains in begging treats, and speeches, from such sort of people. But it must be owned that his Lordship had a singular taste for trifling ceremonies. I remember, when he was Treasurer, he made his white staff be carried by his chair-side by a servant bare-headed; in this, among other things, so very unlike his successor, my Lord Godolphin, who cut his white staff shorter than ordinary, that he might hide it, by taking it into the chair with him.

But if my Lord Rochester believed, as I am persuaded he did, that this order to the Mayor of Bath would have great weight with the Princess, it will be seen, from a short letter from her to me on the occasion, how much he was disappointed.

To Lady Marlborough.—" Dear Mrs. Freeman must give me leave to ask her, if any thing has happened to make her uneasy. I thought she looked to night as if she had the spleen. And I cannot help being in pain whenever I see her so.

" I fancied yesterday, when the Mayor failed in the ceremony of going to church with me, that he was commanded not to do it. I think 'tis a thing to be laughed at. And, if they imagine either to vex me or gain upon me by such sort of usage, they will be mightily disappointed. And I hope these foolish things they do, will every day shew people more and more, what they are, and that they truly deserve the name your faithful Morley has given them."

Another foolish thing, that was done by the same advice, as I suppose, was sending to the minister of St. James's church, where the Princess used to go (while she lived at Berkeley-house) to forbid them to lay the text upon her cushion, or take any more notice of her than of other people. But the minister refusing to obey without some order from the crown in writing, which they did not care to give, that noble design dropt.

After all these notable efforts to subdue the Princess had been employed without success, and when we were got again, as I thought, into a settled, quiet way, at Berkeley-house, my Lord Rochester attempted once more to bring about his purpose, by a stratagem. He came to Sir Benjamin Bathurst, and to others of the Princess's family, insinuating to them, " that if the Princess would put me away, he was persuaded, the Queen would in some time be prevailed upon to let her take me again ;" which was altogether improbable, and indeed ridiculous; because my only pretended fault was being my Lord Marlborough's wife, a fault which I could neither excuse, nor extenuate, nor repent of.

The Princess considered this project as nothing more than a new civil plot of my Lord Rochester's. However she was resolved to leave nothing undone on her part; and therefore, knowing that my Lady Fitzharding could speak more feely to the Queen than any body else, whom she could employ, she sent for her and repeated to her my Lord Rochester's proposal, desiring her to acquaint the Queen, " that from what his Lordship had said, she had been flattering herself, she had mistaken her Majesty's last words; and that if she might hope his Lordship had any ground for his opinion, she should be very ready to give her Majesty any satisfaction of that sort." Upon the delivery of this message, the Queen fell into a great passion, and said, " her sister had not mistaken her, for she never would see her, upon any other terms, than parting with me, not for a time, but for ever," adding, " that she was a Queen, and would be obeyed." Which fine sentence, my Lady Fitzharding confessed, the Queen repeated several times in their conversation; and her Ladyship seemed to find great fault with the Queen's manner of speaking upon that occasion; though excepting this time, my Lady appeared to be a very good courtier.

The Princess, after this, continued at Berkeley-House in a very quiet way. For there was nothing more to be done, unless they would stop her revenue, which doubtless they would have attempted, had they thought it practicable. But my Lord Godolphin was than first commissioner of the Treasury, a man esteemed very useful to the service, and who they knew, would quit upon any such orders. And they could not easily have found a person with qualities fit for that employment, who would have thought it consistent with their honour or safety to take a place, which another had left upon such an account; and at the same time refuse paying the revenue settled by an act of parliament on the next heir to the crown.

I remember nothing more that happened of any moment relating to this Disagreement, till just before the Queen's death.

I shall only observe, that notwithstanding all the harsh things done to the Prince and Princess, they never failed in the least thing, which their friends thought proper for them to do, to show respect to the King, and Queen.

Particularly, on the King's return from Flanders, the Prince sent one of his family to present *his humble duty to his Majesty*, and to acquaint him, *That the Princess having had the misfortune, during his absence, to receive many public marks of the Queen's displeasure, he did not know whether it were proper for him to come to his Majesty, as formerly, without endeavouring first to receive his Majesty's commands, and to know how far it might be agreeable to him.*

The Duke of Gloucester also waited several times on her Majesty, who made a great show of kindness to *him*, and gave him rattles, and several play-things, which were constantly put down in the gazette. And whenever the Duke was sick, she sent a bedcamber woman to Camden-house to enquire how he did. But this compliment was made in so offensive a manner to the Princess, that I have often wondered how any mortal could bear it with the patience she did. For whoever was sent, used to come without ceremony into the room where the Princess herself was, and passing by her, as she stood or sat, without taking more notice of her than if she were a rocker, go directly up to the Duke, and make their speech to him, or to the nurse, as he lay in her lap.

I believe it will be allowed, that there was a good deal of insolence and ill-breeding in this behaviour; and that the Queen might, with safety to all her dignity have found means to satisfy herself about the Duke of Gloucester's health without suffering to be done to the Princess, what no body before ever thought of, and what no private person in this country would bear from another. And yet the return, which the Princess, when she came to the crown, made to this rudeness of the Queen's women, was to give them pensions; a thing which the King himself grew weary of doing some time before he died.

For several months before Queen Mary fell sick of the small-pox, the Princess, thinking herself with child, stayed constantly on one floor, by her physicians' advice lying very much upon a couch to prevent the misfortune of miscarrying. However upon the news of the Queen's dangerous indisposition, she sent a lady of her bed-chamber to present her humble duty to her, and to desire "that her Majesty would believe she was extremely concerned for her illness: adding, that if her Majesty would allow her the happiness of waiting on her, she would notwithstanding the condition she was in, run any hazard for that satisfaction."

This message was delivered to Lady Derby, who having carried it in to her Majesty, came out again some time after, and said, "That the King would send an answer the next day." Accordingly my Lady Derby then wrote to the same Lady, who had brought the message, the following lines,

"MADAM,—I am commanded by the King and Queen to tell you, they desire you would let the Princess know they both thank her for sending and desiring to come: But, it being thought so necessary to keep the Queen as quiet as possible, hope she will defer it.   I am,

          "Madam, Your Ladyship's most humble servant,   "E. DERBY.

"Pray, Madam, present my humble duty to the Princess."

This civil answer, and my Lady Derby's postscript, made me conclude, more than if the college of physicians had told it me, that the disease was mortal. And as I knew that several people, and even one of the Princess's own family, were allowed to see the Queen, I was also fully persuaded, that the deferring the Princess's coming was only to leave room for continuing the quarrel, in case the Queen should chance to recover, or for reconciliation with the King, (if that should be thought convenient) in case of the Queen's death.

During the time of the Queen's illness to her decease, the Princess sent every day to inquire how she did; and once, I am sure, her Majesty heard of it; because my Lady Fitzharding, who was charged with the message, and who had more desire than ordinary to see the Queen, broke in, whether they would or not, and delivered it to her, endeavouring to express in how much concern the Princess was: to which the Queen returned, no answer but a cold thanks. Nor, though she received the sacrament in her illness, did she ever send the least message to the Princess, except that in my Lady Derby's letter, which perhaps her Majesty knew nothing of.

How this conduct to a sister could suit with the character of a devout Queen, I am at a loss to know. For there is nothing more plain in scripture, than the fifth chapter of St. Matthew, v. 23, 24. *Therefore if thou bring thy gift to the altar, and there rememberest that thy brother hath ought against thee, leave there thy gift before the altar, and go thy way: first be reconciled to thy brother, and then come and offer thy gift.*

I will suppose for argument's sake (though I think it scarcely possible), that the Queen might have so wrong an understanding, as to think, she had no reparation to make, and that the Princess had injured her, in not being her slave: yet, even in that case, there was something omitted; for we are taught *to forgive the trespasses against us, as we expect to be forgiven.*

Upon the death of the Queen, the Princess, by advice of my Lord Sunderland and others, wrote the following letter to the King.

"Sir,—I beg your Majesty's favourable acceptance of my sincere and hearty sorrow for your great affliction in the loss of the Queen. And I do assure your Majesty, I am as sensibly touched with this sad misfortune, as if I had never been so unhappy, as to have fallen into her displeasure.

"It is my earnest desire, your Majesty would give me leave to wait upon you, as soon as it can be without inconveniency to you, and without danger of encreasing your affliction, that I may have an opportunity myself not only of repeating this, but of assuring your Majesty of my real intentions to omit no occasion of giving you constant proofs of my sincere respect and concern for your person and interest, as becomes,   Sir,

"Your Majesty's most affectionate sister and servant,   "Anne."

The King had sense enough to know, that it would be impossible to continue any longer an open difference with the Princess, without exposing himself to daily slights, and a manifest disregard for his sovereign pleasure; for he could not hope that the nobility of England would be hindered, now the Queen was dead, from paying respect to a Princess, who was next heir to him by Act of Parliament, and who, if title by blood had taken place, would have had the crown before him; and he was well aware, that every body, who had a mind to shew they did not care for him, would certainly do it by making their court to her.

Quickly after this letter, therefore, the Princess, with the King's consent, and at a time which he appointed, waited on him at Kensington, and was received with extraordinary civility.

And now, it being publicly known, that the quarrel was made up, nothing was to be seen but crowds of people, of all sorts, flocking to Berkeley-house, to pay their respects to the Prince and Princess: a sudden alteration, which, I remember, occasioned the half-witted Lord Caernarvon to say one night to the Princess, as he stood close by her, in the circle, " I hope your Highness will remember that I came to wait upon you, when none of this company did;" which caused a great deal of mirth.

I never heard of any body that opposed this reconciliation, except my Lord Portland. But the person who wholly managed the affair between the King Princess was my Lord Sunderland. He had, upon all occasions relating to her, shewed himself a man of sense and breeding; and before there was any thought of the Queen's dying had designed to use his utmost endeavours to make up the breach; in which, however, I am persuaded he could not have succeeded during the Queen's life. Her death made it easy to him (for the reasons I have mentioned) to bring the King to a reconcilement; and he also persuaded the King to give the Princess St. James's House.

But this and some other favours granted her, at his Lordship's request, were only to save appearances, and for political views. It was very evident that the King did not care, any real respect should be shewn to her Highness. For though to his death she never omitted any thing that was due to him from her, and, by his order, went several times to wait on him at Kensington, no ceremony was observed to her, more than to any other Lady; till the thing had caused some discourse in town. After which my Lord Jersey waited upon her down stairs once or twice, but not oftner. If any body ever came to meet her, it was a page of the back-stairs, or some person whose face was not known. And the Princess, upon these occasions, has waited an hour and a half, just upon the same foot with the rest of the company; and not the least excuse was made for it.

I confess, for my own part, that in the point of *respect to the King (and to the Queen when living)* I thought the Princess did a great deal too much; and it often made me very uneasy. For I could not endure to have her do any thing, that I could not have done in her place. And all the friends I ever had in my life would not have prevailed with me to take any one step, the Princess did, during the quarrel, except the first letter she wrote to the Queen, and the last message of offering to come to her in her sickness. But a letter which the Princess, after the reconcilement, wrote to the King upon the taking of Namur, gave me, I think, more concern than any other instance of her *respectfulness;* though it was advised by three Lords, whose judgments all the world valued. It ran thus,

"Sir,—Though I have been unwilling to give you the trouble of a letter upon any other occasion, yet upon one so glorious to your Majesty as the taking of Namur, I hope you will give me leave to congratulate your good success, which don't please me so much upon any other account, as for the satisfaction, that I am sensible your Majesty must needs feel in this great addition to the reputation of your arms. And I beg leave, Sir, to assure you, that as nobody is more nearly concerned in your interests, so no body wishes more heartily for your happiness and prosperity at home than "Your &c. "Anne."

This letter (which seemed to me so unbecoming the Princess to write) served no other purpose but to give the King an opportunity of shewing his brutal disregard for the writer; for he never returned any answer to it, nor so much as a civil message.

Your Lordship has had some specimens of the manner, in which his Majesty treated the Prince of Denmark before the quarrel. I shall now give you one, of his behaviour to him after the reconcilement.

The King's birth-day coming just after the news of the King of Denmark's death, the Prince, who had a great tenderness for his brother, was extremely uneasy at the thought of putting on colours so soon. And the Princess knowing that it had been the custom in former reigns, to wait upon the King, on a birth-day, without coloured clothes, when the mourning was very deep, found means to get my Lord Albemarle to ask the King's leave, that the Prince might be admitted, in his mourning, to wish his Majesty joy. The answer was, "That the King would not see him, unless he came in his colours;" and the Prince was persuaded to comply, though he did it with great uneasiness.

I believe I could fill as many sheets, as I have already written, with relating the brutalities, that were done to the Prince and Princess in that reign. The King was indeed so ill-natured and so little polished by education, that neither in great things nor in small had he the manners of a gentleman. I shall give you an instance of his worse than vulgar behaviour at his own table, when the Princess dined with him.

It was in the beginning of his reign, and when she was with child of the Duke of Gloucester. There happened to be a plate of pease, the first that had been seen that year. The King, without offering the Princess the least share of them, eat them every one up himself. Whether he offered any to the Queen, I cannot say; but he might do that safely enough, for he knew, she durst not touch them. The Princess confessed, when she came home, she had so much mind to the pease, that she was afraid to look at them, and yet could hardly keep her eyes off them.

But I shall conclude this subject of the King's conduct towards the Princess, with some facts of a deeper concern to her than those incivilities I have just mentioned, and they will show how rightly she judged, when she formerly refused to leave the affair of her maintenance to his generosity.

When the Duke of Gloucester was arrived at the age to be put into men's hands, the King insinuated to such members of the Parliament as he knew were desirous to have the Duke handsomely settled, that it would require near 50,000l. a year. And, at the same time, he promised other persons, whom, he knew it would please, that he would pay Queen Mary in France her settlement, which was also 50,000l. a year. And these steps he took, in order to obtain an addition of a 100,000l. a year to his civil list.

The addition was granted, yet he never paid one shilling to the Queen: And, as to the Duke, the King not only kept him in women's hands a good while after the new revenue was granted, but, when his Highness's family was settled, would give him no more than 15,000l. a year. Nay, of this small allowance, he refused to advance one quarter, though it was absolutely wanted to buy plate and furniture: So that the Princess was forced to be at that expence herself.

But this was not all. The King (influenced, I suppose, in this particular, by my Lord Sunderland) sent the Princess word, that, though he intended to put in all the preceptors, he would leave it to her to chuse the rest of the servants, except one, who was to be Deputy Governor and Gentleman of the Duke's bed chamber, (which was Mr. Sayers.)

This message was so humane, and of so different an air from any thing the Princess had been used to, that it gave her an extreme pleasure; and she immediately set herself to provide proper persons, and of the most consideration, for the several places. Mr. Boscawen and Secretary Vernon's son were to be grooms of the bed-chamber; the sons of the Earls of Bridgewater and

Berkeley were to be pages of honour, and so on. In the meantime the King was in no haste to finish the affair of the Duke's establishment; and a little before he left England to go make the campaign, told my Lord Marlborough, (who was now restored to the army, and was to be Governor to the Duke of Gloucester) " that he would send a list, from abroad, of the servants he would have in the Duke's family," not in the least regarding the former message, he had sent to the Princess; which my Lord observing, took the liberty to put his Majesty in mind of it, adding, that the Princess, upon the credit of that message, had engaged her promises to several persons; and that, not to be able to perform those promises, would be so great a mortification, as he hoped his Majesty would not give her, at a time, when any thing of trouble might do her prejudice, she being then with child. Hereupon the King fell into a great passion, and said, " she should not be Queen before her time, and he would make the list of what servants the Duke should have."

The King was so peremptory, that my Lord Marlborough could say no more, and had no expedient left, but to get my Lord Albemarle to try to bring him to reason; which his Lordship promised to do. And accordingly he took my Lord Marlborough's list of the persons the Princess had chosen, and carried it with him into Holland. In conclusion that list was approved, with very few alterations. But this was, without question, not so much owing to the King's goodness, or my Lord Albemarle's persuasions, (though I believe his Lordship did take pains in this matter) as to the happy choice the Princess had made of the servants. For the King, upon cool consideration, must perceive, that he could not strike out of the list a greater number than he did, without hurting himself, more than the Princess. He only made my Lord Raby's brother an equerry, and appointed, to be gentlemen waiters, two or three persons, who had served the late Queen in such like stations, and had pensions on that account. And it was to save this money that the King did so ungentlemanlike a thing, as to force the Princess to fail in some of her engagements. And he gave afterwards another remarkable proof of his good management; for upon the news of the Duke of Gloucester's death, he sent orders, by the very first post, to have all his servants discarded; a diligence of frugality, which was surely not very decent in a king. It was by the contrivance of Lord Marlborough, assisted by Lord Albemarle, that the servants received their salaries to the quarter-day after the Duke died.

And now, after all I have related of the King, and after so much dislike, as I have expressed of his character and conduct, you will perhaps hardly believe me, in what I am going to say: Yet, your Lordship *will* believe me; for you will judge of my heart, by the make and temper of your own. When the King came to die, I felt nothing of that satisfaction, which I once thought I should have had upon this occasion. And my Lord and Lady Jersey's writing and sending perpetually to give an account, as his breath grew shorter and shorter, filled me with horror. I thought I would lose the best employment in any court, sooner than act so odious a part. And the King, who had given me so much cause to hate him, in that condition I sincerely pitied: So little is it in my nature to retain resentment against any mortal, (how unjust soever he may have been) in whom *the will to injure* is no more.

§ II.—THE King died, and the Princess of Denmark took his place. This elevation of my mistress to the throne brought me into a new scene of life, and into a new sort of consideration with all those, whose attention, either by curiosity or ambition, was turned to politics and the court. Hitherto my favour with her Royal Highness, though it had sometimes furnished matter of conversation to the public, had been of no moment to the affairs of the nation, she herself having no share in the councils, by which they were managed. But from this time, I began to be looked upon as a person of consequence, without whose approbation, at least, neither places, nor pensions, nor honours were bestowed by the crown. The intimate friendship, with which the Queen was known to honour me, afforded a plausible foundation for this opinion : And I believe therefore, it will be a surprise to many, to be told, that the first important step, which her Majesty took, after her accession to the government, was against my wishes and inclination : I mean, " her throwing herself and her affairs almost entirely into the hands of the tories."

I shall dwell the longer, and be the more particular upon the subject of my disagreement with her Majesty about parties, that I may expose the injustice of those whigs, who, after the great change in 1710, accused me of being the ruin of their cause ; a cause, that, in her reign, would have been always too low, to be capable of a fall, but for the zeal and diligence, with which I seized every opportunity to raise and establish it ; which, in the end, proved the ruin of my favour with her Majesty.

The Queen had from her infancy imbibed the most unconquerable prejudices against the whigs. She had been taught to look upon them all, not only as republicans, who hated the very shadow of regal authority, but as implacable enemies to the church of England. This aversion to the whole party had been confirmed by the ill usage she had met with from her sister and King William, which though perhaps more owing to Lord Rochester, than to any man then living, was now to be all charged to the account of the whigs. And Prince George, her husband, who had also been ill treated, in that reign, threw into the scale his resentments.

On the other hand, the tories had the advantage, not only of the Queen's early prepossession in their favour, but of their having assisted her in the late reign, in the affair of her *settlement*. It was indeed evident, that they had done this, more in opposition to King William, than from any real respect for the Princess of Denmark. But still they had served her. And the winter before she came to the crown, they had in the same spirit of opposition to the King, and in prospect of his death, paid her more than usual civilities and attendance.

It is no great wonder therefore, all these things considered, that as soon as she was seated in the throne, the tories (whom she usually called by the agreeable name of the church-party) became the distinguished objects of the royal favour.

Dr. Sharp, Archbishop of York, was pitched upon by herself to preach her coronation sermon, and to be her chief counsellor in church-matters; and her privy-council was filled with tories. My Lord Normanby (soon after Duke of Buckingham) the Earls of Jersey and Nottingham, Sir Edward Seymour, with many others of the high-fliers, were brought into places ; Sir Nathan Wright was continued in possession of the great seal of England, and the Earl of Rochester in the Lieutenancy of Ireland. These were men, who had all a wonderful zeal for the church ; a sort of public merit that eclipsed all other in the eyes of the Queen. And I am firmly persuaded, that notwithstanding her extraordinary affection for me, and the entire devotion which my Lord Marlborough and my Lord Godolphin had for many years shown to her service, they would not have had so great a share of her favour and confidence, if they had not been reckoned in the number of the tories.

The truth is, though both these Lords had always the real interest of the nation at heart, and had given proof of this, by their conduct in their several employments, in the late reign, they had been educated in the persuasion, that the high-church party were the best friends to the constitution, both of church and state ; nor were they perfectly undeceived by experience.

For my own part, I had not the same prepossessions. The *word CHURCH* had never any charm for *me*, in the mouths of those, who made the most noise with it ; for I could not perceive that they gave any other distinguishing proof of their regard for the *thing*, than a frequent use of the *word*, like a spell to enchant weak minds ; and a persecuting zeal against dissenters, and against those real friends of the church, who would not admit that *persecution* was agreeable to its doctrine. And as to state-affairs, many of these churchmen seemed to me, to have no fixed principles at all, having endeavoured, during the last reign, to undermine that very government, which they had contributed to establish.

I was heartily sorry therefore, that, for the sake of such churchmen, others should be removed from their employments, who had been firm to the principles of the Revolution, and whom I thought much more likely to support the Queen, and promote the welfare of our country, than the wrong-headed politicians that succeeded them.

I resolved therefore, from the very beginning of the Queen's reign, to try whether I could not by degrees make impressions in her mind more favourable to the whigs ; and though my instances with her had not at first any considerable effect, I believe, I may venture to say, it was, in some measure, owing to them, that her Majesty did, against her own inclinations, continue several of this party in office. And it is well known, that the Queen, in the first year of her reign, had determined to create four new peers, the Lords Granville, Guernsey, Gower and Conway, I prevailed that Mr. Hervey (the present Earl of Bristol) might be a *fifth*, in spite of the opposition of the tories, and especially of the *four* above named ; who for a while refused to accept of the peerage, if Mr. Hervey, a whig, were admitted to the same honour.

But how difficult a task I prescribed to myself, when I undertook to moderate her Majesty's partiality to the tories, and to engage her to a better opinion of their opposites, will abundantly appear from the following letter, which I had the honour to receive from her, about half a year after her accession to the throne.

"*St. James's, Saturday the 24th October*—I am very glad to find by my dear Mrs. Freeman's, that I was blest with yesterday, that she liked *my speech*, but I cannot help being extremely concerned, you are so partial to the whigs, because I would not have you, and your * poor, unfortunate, faithful Morley differ in opinion in the least thing. What I said, when I writ last upon this subject, does not proceed from any insinuations of the other party ; but I know the principles of the church of England, and I know those of the whigs, and it is that, and no other reason, which makes me think as I do, of the last. And upon my word, my dear Mrs. Freeman, you are mightily mistaken in your notion of a true wig : For the character, you give of them, does not in the least

* The Queen began to stile herself after this manner, upon the death of the Duke of Gloucester.

belong to them, but to the church. But I will say no more on this subject, only beg, for my poor sake, that you would not show more countenance to those, you seem to have so much inclination for, than to the church party. Since you have staid so long at Windsor, I wish now for your own sake, that you would stay till after *my Lord Mayor's Day;* for if you are in town, *you can't avoid going to the show,* and being in the country is a just excuse; and, I think, one would be glad of any to avoid so troublesome a business. I am this time in great haste, and therefore can say no more to my dear dear Mrs. Freeman, but that I am most passionately her's."*

As my early zeal for the whigs is incontestably manifest from what her Majesty here says to me, so, I think, it will be no less evident to any one who reflects on my situation at that time, that this zeal could proceed from nothing but conviction of the goodness of the cause I espoused.

For, as to private interest, the whigs could have done nothing for my advantage more than the tories. I needed not the assistance of either to ingratiate myself with the Queen. She had both before and since her accession given the most unquestionable proofs, that she considered me, not only as a most faithful servant, but as her dear friend. I have mentioned nothing of her extreme goodness to me since the breaking out of the quarrel between her sister and herself, that I might not interrupt the relation of that matter in which my chief aim was the justification of my mistress's conduct and my own upon that occasion. Her letters to me afterwards, of which I have great numbers still by me, were in the same strain of tenderness as those you have read ; and upon her coming to the crown, she had not only made me her Groom of the Stole, and Keeper of the Privy Purse, but had given the command of the army to my Lord Marlborough, and the Treasurer's Staff to my Lord Godolphin, to whose son my eldest daughter was married.

It is plain therefore that I could have no motive of private interest to bias me to the whigs. Every body must see, that, had I consulted the oracle about the choice of a party, it would certainly have directed me to go with the stream of my mistress's inclination and prejudices. This would have been the surest way to secure my favour with her.

Nor had I any particular obligations to the whigs that should bend me to their side rather than to the other. On the contrary, they had treated me very hardly, and I had reason to look upon them as my personal enemies, at the same time that I saw the tories ready to compliment me, and to pay me court. Even the pride of my Lord Rochester condescended to write me a very fine piece, when my Lady Charlotte Beverwaert died, that his daughter, my Lady Dalkeith, might be a lady of the bedchamber in her place. I confess indeed, I was not a little surprised at this application from his Lordship. I thank God, I have had experience enough of my own temper to be very sure I can forgive any injury, when the person, from whom I have received it, shows any thing like repentance. But could I ever be so unfortunate, as to persecute ano-

---

* The Queen very seldom dated her letters fully, and the year is not mentioned in the date of this, but it is evident from the contents, that it was written in 1702, the first year of her Majesty's reign ; for she went that year to my Lord Mayor's Show, nothing but *her* going could have made it unavoidable for *me* to go, if I were in town. And whoever will give themselves the trouble of the enquiry, will find that the 24th of October fell that year on a Saturday, and that the Queen made her speech to the Parliament a few days before.

ther without cause, as my Lord Rochester did me, I am confident, that even want of bread could not induce me to ask a favour of that person. But surely his Lordship had something very uncommon in his temper.

What induced him to the present condescension, was, I suppose, his late experience, that I did not make use of my influence with the Queen, to gratify any personal pique or resentment. For upon the Queen's accession to the throne, Lady Hyde had spoke to me, that she might be a lady of the bed-chamber; and I had served her very sincerely and effectually. For though the Queen did not like her, yet, as her Majesty had been pleased to forgive the ill behaviour of my Lord Rochester to her, during the reigns of King Charles, King James, and Queen Mary, I thougt it reasonable that his son's wife should be a lady of the bed-chamber. There was, in truth, a particular pleasure in serving my Lady Hyde in this instance on her own account; for in my life I never saw any mortal have such a passion for any thing, as she had to be in that post. While the thing was depending, she had so much concern upon her, that she never spoke to me upon the subject without blushing. And after it was granted, she made me more expressions, than ever I had from any body on any occasion. Among other compliments, I had this letter from her.

Monday Morning —" I have been three times in the drawing room, in hopes to meet your Ladyship there, that I might myself tell you, how extreme sensible I am of your Ladyship's favour to me. You will add another, if you will forgive my impatience, that cannot stay longer without thanking you myself, though Mrs. Lowther has undertaken for me. I am very happy in my request being granted, and your Ladyship may depend, any command of your's shall be obeyed, for I will not, without your leave, brag even to my Lady Hariotte, who did me the favour to speak to your Ladyship. I am not good at saying much, but I am sure it will be a pleasure to me to shew you in every thing I can, how faithfully and sincerely I am

  " Your Ladyship's humble servant,   "J. Hyde."

In what manner this Lady treated me afterwards, is not worth the while to mention.

As to my Lord Rochester's request in behalf of my Lady Dalkeith, it could not be granted; because in reality there was no vacancy. The Queen had resolved to have no more than ten ladies, and the number was complete. There had indeed been eleven for some short time; but this had been occasioned by the Duchess of Somerset's declining to accept one of these places when it was offered her at the settling of the Queen's family, and soon after desiring to have it, when they were all filled. As she was the first protestant Duchess of England, I persuaded the Queen to be pleased, in compliment to her Grace, to have eleven ladies for the little time Lady Charlotte Beverwaert had to live, who was then irrecoverably ill. So that when her Majesty complied, it was with full purpose that the number of her ladies should be only ten after Lady Charlotte's death. And this answer having been given to several others who had solicited to succeed Lady Charlotte, my Lord Rochester could have no reason to be offended, that the like excuse was made to him, with regard to his daughter.

I have been the more particular on this affair, that it may appear, the refusal my Lord Rochester met with was not owing to any resentment of mine, against him or his family. And I do assure you most sincerely, that I could so entirely have forgotten all his Lordship's ill treatment of me, as to have acted in concert and friendship with him, if I had thought he would have followed the Queen's true interests. But the gibberish of that party about non-resistance and passive-obedience and hereditary right, I could not think to forebode any good to my Mistress, whose title rested upon a different foundation. On the other hand, the principles professed by those called whigs seemed to me rational, entirely tending to the preservation of the liberties of the subject, and no way to the prejudice of the church as by law established; for which, I believe I may without vanity venture to say, I had at least as much respect, as the Duke of Buckingham or Sir Edward Seymour. And as this was really my way of thinking concerning the two parties, it would have been contrary to the frankness of my temper and to the obligations of that friendship with which the Queen honoured me, not to have told her my sentiments without reserve. Nay I had her express command so to do. She had often urged me to it, in almost the same terms she uses in a letter of her own hand-writing, which I have now before me.

" You can never give me any greater proof of your friendship than in telling me your mind freely in all things, which I do beg you to do, &c."

I did therefore speak very freely and very frequently to her Majesty upon the subject of whig and tory, according to my conception of their different views and principles. It was at first to little effect; and perhaps I should never have succeeded so far as I did, if the leaders of the tories had not, by the heat and agitation with which they over-acted their part, exposed that monopolizing ambition, which ought to have been better concealed under the cloak of zeal for the church.

The church of England, one would naturally think, could not be in any *immediate* danger of perishing under the care of such *a nursing mother* as the Queen, whose affection to it was never doubted, and who, for it's better security, had chosen it's most renowned champions to be of her ministry and council. Nevertheless in the very first new Parliament, after her Majesty's accession, it was thought necessary with all diligence to provide new strength, new supports for this flourishing church, as if it had been in the most tottering and declining condition.

One cannot better represent the noble spirit, with which the zealots began their play than by transcribing some part of the Commons' address to the Queen, in answer to her most gracious speech at the opening of the sessions.

" ———— Your Majesty has been always a most illustrious ornament to this church, and has been exposed to great hazards for it, and therefore we promise ourselves, that, in your Majesty's reign, we shall see it perfectly restored to its due rights and privileges, and secured in the same to posterity ; which is only to be done by divesting those men of the power, who have shown they want not the will to destroy it."

The Queen in her speech had declared her resolution to defend and main-tain the church as by law established. Of *this* they tell her they have no doubt, after her repeated assurances. But *this* was not enough. So illustrious an ornament of the church must not content herself with protecting it in its *legal* rights, but she must contribute to restore it to its *due* rights, that is, she must restore tories and high-churchmen to their *divine* rights and privileges of possessing all the civil offices in the state, and being the only men elected to serve in Parliament, to the exclusion of all whigs and low-churchmen, who being enemies of the church, and having a will to destroy it, must be divested of the power to execute their malice.

That this was the meaning of the address I believe no body doubts, and the *occasional conformity bill*, which in consequence of this zeal for the church, was soon brought into Parliament, did not aim at excluding from employments the *occasional* conformists only, but all those *constant* conformists too, who could not relish the high-church nonsense of promoting religion by persecution. For as the tories were well acquainted with her Majesty's entire devotion to the church, they designed this *bill*, as a *test*, whereby she might certainly distinguish its friends from its foes; and they doubted not but she would reckon among the latter whoever should oppose so religious a scheme.

The bill, as every body knows, was carried triumphantly through the House of Commons; and the Prince of Denmark (though himself an occasional conformist) was persuaded to vote for it, in the house of Lords. However it miscarried there (I forget how) to the great disappointment and mortification of the party. Nay it began to be suspected that some of the chief men at court were not so zealous in the good cause as they should be. My Lord Rochester was, I think, the first of the tory leaders that discovered a deep discontent with the Queen and her administration. Before the end of the year he resigned the lieutenancy of Ireland in great wrath, upon her Majesty's being so unreasonable as to press him to go thither to attend the affairs of that kingdom, which greatly needed his presence. For as the revenue, which had been formerly granted was out, it was necessary to call a Parliament in order to another supply; and a Parliament could not be held without a Lord Lieutenant. But when the Queen represented these things to him he told her with insolence, the *he would not go into Ireland, though she would give the country to him and his son;* so that he seems to have accepted the post only that he might reign in Ireland by the ministry of his brother Keightley, as he hoped to do in England, in person. Nor could he, after his resignation, overcome his anger so far as to wait upon the Queen or to go to council; which she observing ordered, after some time, that he should no more be summoned, saying, " it was not reasonable my Lord Rochester should come to council only when he pleased."

Perhaps his Lordship's unwillingness to leave England might proceed from his zeal for the church, and from his fears lest it should be betrayed in his absence. But it was generally thought, and I believe with good reason, that the true source of his dissatisfaction was the Queen's not making him her sole governor and director, and my Lord Godolphin's being preferred before him for the treasury; Which, if true, affords a remarkable instance, how much self-love and self-conceit can blind even a man of sense; for such, by his party at least, he was esteemed to be. I don't wonder that he should like power (it is what most people are fond of) or that being related to the Queen he should expect a particular consideration. This was very natural and very reasonable, if he had behaved himself to her as he ought: But when one considers, that his relation to her was by such a sort of accident, and that his conduct had been so very extraordinary, 'tis an amazing thing that he should imagine, he was to domineer over the Queen and every body else, as he did over his own family.

Whether the church was in any danger or not *before*, it could not be questioned by any good churchman, but it *now* began to be in some peril when my Lord Rochester was no longer in place, nor in council.

The bill against occasional conformity was revived by the tories the next sessions of Parliament; which proceeding, whatever regard it might show for the church, did certainly show little respect or gratitude to the Queen, who had hitherto showered her favours upon the party.   For her Majesty having been informed, that this bill had alarmed a great part of her subjects, who were otherwise perfectly well affected to her gouernment, and no less able than zealous to assist her in carrying on the war against the common enemy, had endeavoured in her speech, by the warmest expressions, to dissuade the Parliament from this measure, as it might prove a source of fatal divisions at home, where union and harmony were so necessary in order to the success of our affairs abroad.

But the interest of the *church*, that is, of *high-churchman*, was to be preferred before the interest of the Queen or of the nation, or the preservation of the liberties of Europe.   The bill was therefore brought in again ; but, though it had once more an easy passage through the House of Commons, it met with the same fate as the year before in the House of Lords.

This new blow to the church was soon followed by another, the removal of Lord Jersey and Sir Edward Seymour from their employments ; and about the same time Lord Nottingham resigned his place of Secretary of State, because the whigs were too much favoured.

The whigs did indeed begin to be favoured, and with good reason. For when they saw that my Lord Marlborough prosecuted the common cause with such hearty diligence and such unexpected success, they notwithstanding the partiality which had been shown to their opposites, universally forgot their resentments, aud no longer considering themselves as an oppressed party, ran in with the loudest acclamations, extolling his merit and services: And as the trade and money of the nation were chiefly in the hands of those, who espoused the cause, in which the ministry were then engaged, it is no wonder that my Lord Godolphin began to pay them as much regard as the times and the Queen's prejudices would permit him to do.

The church in the mean while, it must be confessed, was in a deplorable condition.   The Earls of Rochester, Jersey, and Nottingham, and Sir Edward Seymour out of place, and the whigs coming into favour.   It was resolved therefore the next sessions of Parliament to tack the occasional conformity bill to the money bill, a resolution which showed the spirit of the party in it's true light.   But it happened that my Lord Marlborough, in the summer before the Parliament met, gained the battle of Blenheim.   This was an unfortunate accident ; and by the visible dissatisfaction of some people on the news of it, one would have imagined, that instead of beating the French, he had beat the church. And I cannot here omit one remarkable instance of true party spirit in the tories on this occasion.   My Lord Marlborough, before he had had sufficient opportunity of showing the greatness of the general, had, for his first successes in the war, been complimented by this very House of Commons, as the *retriever of the glory of the English nation*, being then reputed a high churchman. But now that he was thought to look towards the moderate party, his *complete victory* at Blenheim, was in the address of congratulation to the Queen, ridiculously paired with Sir George Rook's *drawn battle* with the French at sea.

However, neither the glory of this victory, nor, the important consequences of it, could be hid, even from the eyes of those who would have been the most willing not to see them.   The power of France was broken by it to a great degree, and the liberties and peace of Europe were in a fair way to be established upon firm and lasting foundations.   The less violent part of the tories therefore could not be prevailed with to hazard these great and pleasing hopes, by tacking them to the fortune of the *occasional conformity bill.* The tack was rejected by the majority of the members, even of this House of Commons, so rich in tories and high churchmen. And though the bill by itself was afterwards passed in that House, it was again thrown out by the Lords.

The last great wound given to the church this year, was by the Queen's taking the privy seal from the Duke of Buckingham.

And next year I prevailed with her Majesty to take the great seal from Sir Nathan Wright, a man despised by all parties, of no use to the crown, and whose weak and wretched conduct in the court of *chancery,* had almost brought his very office into contempt. His removal however was a great loss to the church, for which he had ever been a warm stickler. And this loss was the more sensibly felt, as his successor, my Lord Cowper, was not only of the whig-party, but of such abilities and integrity, as brought a new credit to it in the nation.

But, what was worse than all these misfortunes, the majority of the House of Commons in the new Parliament of 1705, proved to be whig.

No wonder if, in these sad circumstances, a loud and piteous cry was raised upon the extreme danger of the poor church. A doleful piece, penned by some of the zealots of the party, and called *The Memorial of the Church of England,* was printed and spread abroad, setting forth her melancholy condition and distress ; and much lamentation it occasioned. But what remedy ? There could be no hope of getting an *occasional conformity bill* passed in this Parliament. One expedient still remained ; and this was, to invite the Princess Sophia of Hanover, the present King's grandmother, to come over and defend the church. Her presence here, though she would not probably, as being a Lutheran, be very zealous for a bill against occasional conformists, yet might happily prove a means to hinder the whigs from bringing in popery and the pretender. A motion was therefore made in the house of Lords for this invitation ; and the necessity of it was urged with great strength of argument by the Earls of Rochester and Nottingham, and the other grave men of the party. Not that they had the least hope or the least desire to carry their point, but being well assured that the Queen would never consent to such an invitation, nor pardon her ministers if they encouraged the design, this was a notable stratagem to ruin them, either with her Majesty, or with the nation ; for if in compliance with her prejudices they opposed this motion, it was to be hoped it would draw the public odium upon them, as declared enemies to the protestant succession.

This hopeful scheme however did not succeed. The whigs opposed the invitation, and yet preserved their credit, to the great mortification of the other party. I know that my Lord Godolphin, and other great men, were much reflected upon by some well disposed persons, for not laying hold of this opportunity, which the tories put into their hands, of more effectually securing the succession to the crown in the house of Hanover. But those of the whigs, whose anger against the minister was raised on this account, little knew how inpracticable the project of *invitation* was, and that the attempt would have only served to make the Queen discard her ministry, to the ruin of the common cause of these kingdoms, and of all Europe. I had often tried her Majesty upon this subject; and when I found that she would not hear of the immediate successor's coming over, had pressed her that she would at least invite hither the young Prince of Hanover, who was not to be her immediate successor, and that she would let him live here as her son: but her Majesty would listen to no proposal of this kind in any shape whatsoever.

To give a full answer to all objections against the ministers' conduct with regard to this matter, I shall here relate a transaction that passed three years afterwards, which will show not only the insincerity of the tories in their zeal for the house of Hanover, when they moved for the Princess Sophia's being invited hither, but how insuperably averse the Queen was to suffer the pre- sence of any of that family.

My Lord Haversham, a great speech-maker, and publisher of his speeches, and who was become the mouth of the party for any extraordinary alarm, was sent privately by the tories to the Queen to acquaint her with a discovery, which they pretended to have made, of a terrible design formed by the whigs to bring over one of the House of Hanover, and to force this upon her whether she would or not. Now can any thing be more curious than such a message from the tories, and by such a messenger? For my Lord Haversham was the man who had moved for the Princess Sophia's coming over as a thing neces- sary for the preservation of the Protestant religion. But *now* any design of inviting hither one of that family was of so frightful a nature, that it must be esteemed meritorious to give early notice of the danger, I shall make no more comment upon this proceeding, but transcribe a part of the Queen's letter to the Duke of Marlborough upon this occasion.

July 22d, 1708.—"———— I cannot end this without giving you an account in short of a visit I have had from Lord Haversham. He told me his business was to let me know, there was certainly a design laying between the whigs and some great men, to have an address made in the next sessions of Parlia- ment for inviting the Electoral Prince over to settle here, and that he would certainly come to make a visit as soon as the campaign was over, and there was nothing for me to do to prevent my being forced to this (as I certainly would,) but my shewing myself to be Queen, and making it my own act. I told him, if this matter should be brought into Parliament, whoever proposed it, whether whig or tory, I should look upon neither of them as my friends, nor would ever make any invitation neither to the young man nor his father, nor his grandmother.

"———— What I have to say to you upon this subject, at this time, is to beg you would find whether there is any design where you are, that the young man should make a visit in the winter, and contrive some way to put any such thought out of their head, that the difficulty may not be brought upon me of refusing him leave to come, if he should ask it; or forbidding him to come, if he should attempt it: For one of these two things *I must do,* if either he or his father should have any desires to have him see this country, it being a thing *I cannot bear,* to have any successor here, though but for a week. And there- fore I shall depend upon you to do every thing on the other side of the water to prevent this mortification from coming upon her, that is, and ever will be, most sincerely, &c."

To return to the motion for inviting the Princess Sophia. It was upon this occasion that the Queen gave the first indications of any thing like a real re- concilement to the whigs. For though she had been prevailed with to ex- press a desire, that the Parliament would avoid measures tending to create di- visions and animosities at home (meaning the occasional conformity bill), yet you will see by the following letters from her Majesty to me, how much she leaned all along, in her inclination, to the tories, and even to those very measures she would have dissuaded them from; and which she only thought unseasonable at that time.

Friday morning.—" I give my dear Mrs. Freeman many thanks for her long letter, and am truly sensible of the extreme kindness you express in it; and in turn, to ease your mind, I must tell you, *Mr. Bromley will be disappointed, for the Prince does not intend to go to the House, when the Bill of Occasional Conformity is brought in ;* but at the same time that I think him very much in the right not to vote in it, I shall not have the worse opinion of any of the Lords that are for it; for though *I should have been very glad, it had not been brought into the House of Commons,* because I would not have had any pretence given for quarrelling ; I can't help thinking, *now it is as good as past there,* it will be *better for the service to have it pass the House of Lords too.* I must own to you, that I never cared to mention any thing of this subject to you, because I knew you would not be of my mind; but since you have given me this occasion, I can't forbear saying, that *that I see nothing like persecution in this Bill. You may think it is a notion Lord Nottingham has put into my head,* but *upon my word it is my own thought.* I am in hopes I shall have one look before you go to St. Alban's, and therefore will say no more now, but will answer your letter more at large some other time ; and only promise my dear Mrs. Freeman faithfully, I will read the *book* she sent me, and beg she would never let difference of opinion hinder us from living together, as we used to do. Nothing shall ever alter your poor Morley, who will live and die with all truth and tenderness your's*.

The following letters from the Queen to me, relate to the Occasional Conformity Bill, when it was intended to tack it to the Money Bill in 1704.

November 17th, 1704.—" ——— I am sure nobody shall endeavour more to promote it [*union*] than you poor, unfortunate, faithful Morley, *who doth not at all doubt of your truth and sincerity to her,* and hopes *her not agreeing in every thing you say* will not be imputed to want of value, esteem, or tender kindness for my dear Mrs. Freeman, it being impossible for any one to be more sincerely another's, than I am your's.

" *St. James's, November the 21st.*—I had just sealed up my letter on *Saturday* night as I received the satisfaction of my dear Mrs. Freeman's of that day's date, but would not open it again, concluding I should have time, either *Sunday* or *yesterday,* to thank you for it. When *Sunday* came I had several hindrances, and *yesterday* I sat down to write, but was hindered by one of the *Scots* people coming to speak with me, or else I should not have been so long without telling you, I am very sorry, you should forbear writing upon the apprehension of your letters being troublesome, *since you know very well they are not, nor never can be so,* but the contrary, to your poor, unfortunate, faithful Morley. Upon what my dear Mrs. Freeman says again concerning the address, I have looked it over again, and cannot for my life see, one can put any other interpretation

---

* It is evident, that this letter, though it bears no other date than Friday morning, was written about the beginning of December, 1703, when the *Occasional Conformity Bill* was brought in by Mr. Bromley. And it is probable, from some words in the letter, that this bill had passed the committee when the Queen wrote.

Lord Nottingham, by whose advice the Queen supposes that I believe her influenced, was then Secretary of State.

The Prince of Denmark did not vote for the bill this year, nor go to the House on this occasion ; so that Mr. Bromley *was disappointed.*

upon that word *pressures*, than what I have done already. As to my saying the church was in some danger in the late reign, I cannot alter my opinion; for though there was no violent thing done, every body that will speak impartially must own, that every thing was leaning towards the whigs, *and whenever that is, I shall think the church beginning to be in danger.*"

But though it appears by these letters that the Queen was not hitherto inwardly converted to the whigs, neither by all that I had been able to say, nor even by the mad conduct of the tacking tories, yet, as I before hinted, their behaviour in the affair of the *invitation* occasioned something like a change in her. She had been present at the debates in the House of Lords upon that subject, and had heard the Duke of Buckingham treat her with great disrespect, urging as an argument for inviting over the Princess Sophia, that the Queen might live till she did not know what she did, and be like a child in the hands of others: and a great deal to the same effect. Such rude treatment from the tories, and the zeal and success of the whigs in opposing a motion, so extremely disagreeable to her, occasioned her to write to me in the following terms.

"———I believe dear Mrs. Freeman and I shall not disagree as we have formerly done: for I am sensible of the services those people have done me that you have a good opinion of, and will countenance them, and am thoroughly convinced of the malice and insolence of *them*, that you have always been speaking against."

And at this same time, her Majesty authorised my Lord Godolphin to give the utmost assurances to the chief men of the whigs, that she would put herself and her affairs into such hands as they should approve, and would do every thing possible for the security of the protestant succession.

But notwithstanding this, it was not till after much solicitation, that her Majesty could be prevailed with, so far to oblige the whigs, as to make my Lord Sunderland, Secretary of State in the room of Sir Charles Hedges. The whigs, after the services they had done, and the assurances the Queen had given them, thought it reasonable to expect, that *one* of the secretaries at least should be such a man as they could place a confidence in. They believed they might trust my Lord Sunderland; and though they did not think him the properest man for the post, yet being my Lord Marlborough's son-in-law, they chose to recommend him to her Majesty, because, as they expressed themselves to me, they imagined it was *driving the nail that would go.*

I must observe here that my Lord Marlborough was not, in his inclination, for this promotion of my Lord Sunderland. I have a letter from him expressing his dislike to the design. But how hard pressed both he and my Lord Godolphin were by the whigs to have it brought to effect, will fully appear by the following letter on the same subject.

"*Grametz, October* 1706,—When I writ my last, I was very full of the spleen; and I think with too much reason. My whole time, to the best of my understanding, has been employed for the public good, as I do assure you I do in the presence of God, neglecting no opportunity of letting 83 * see what I take to be her true interest. It is terrible to go through so much uneasiness. I do not say this to flatter any party, for I will never do it, let the consequence be what it will. For, as parties, they are both in the wrong. But 'tis certain 79 and his adherents are not to be trusted. So that 83 has no choice, but that

---

* The Queen.

of employing those who will carry on the war and support 91·*. And if any other method is taken I know we shall go into confusion. Now this being the case, I leave you to judge, whether I am dealt kindly with? I do not say this for any other end, but to have your justice and kindness; for in that will consist my future happiness. I am sure I would venture a thousand lives, if I had them, to procure ease and happiness to the Queen. And yet no number of men could persuade me to act as a minister in what was not my opinion. So that I shall never fail in speaking my mind very freely. And as my opinion is, that the tackers and all the adherents of 73 are not for carrying on the war, which is for the true Interest of the Queen and kingdom, you may depend I shall never join with any but such as I think will serve her and the true interest of our country with all their hearts. And if the war continues but one year longer with success, I hope it will not be in any body's power to make the Queen's business uneasy. And then I shall be glad to live as quiet as possible, and not envy the governing men, who would then I believe think better of 90 and 91 † than they now do. And I will own frankly to you, that the jealousy some of your friends have, that 90 and 91 do not act sincerely, makes me so weary, that, were it not for my gratitude for 83, and concern for 91, I would now retire and never serve more. For I have had the good luck to deserve better from all Englishmen, than to be suspected for not being in the true interest of my country; which I am in, and ever will be, without being of a faction. And this principle shall govern me for the little remainder of my life. I must not think of being popular; but I shall have the satisfaction of my going to the grave with the opinion of having acted, as became an honest man. And if I have your esteem and love, I should think myself entirely happy. Having writ thus far I have received your two letters of the 20th and 21st, which confirm me in my opinion before. And since the resolution is taken to vex and ruin 91, because 83 has not complied with what was desired for 117 ‡, I shall from henceforward despise all mankind, and think there is no such thing as virtue. For I know with what zeal 91 has pressed 83 in that matter. I do pity him, and shall always love him as long as I live; and never be a friend to any that can be his enemy.

"I have writ my mind every freely to 83 ‖, on this occasion, so that whatever misfortune may happen, I shall have a quiet mind, having done what I thought my duty. And as for the resolution of making me uneasy, I believe they will not have much pleasure in that, for as I have not set my heart on having justice done me, I shall not be disappointed; nor will I be ill used by any man."

I shall here add a letter of my own to the Queen on the same subject; and the rather, because it not only confirms what I have said of her Majesty's *unwillingness to oblige the whigs*, but shews that as much as I opposed the tories, I was no enemy to the *church* they *talked* of, so far as any thing *real* and *excellent* was meant by that word; and because it contains so just a prediction of the usage, the Queen afterwards met with, when she fell into the hands of the high church party.

" By the letter I had from your Majesty this morning, and the great weight you put upon the difference betwixt the word notion and nation in my letter, I am only made sensible (as by many other things) that you were in a great disposition to complain of me, since to this moment, I cannot for my life see

---

* Lord Godolphin.   † Lord Marlborough and Lord Godolphin.
‡ Lord Sunderland.   ‖ The Queen.

any essential difference betwixt these two words, as to the sense of my letter, the true meaning of which was only to let your Majesty know, with that faithfulness and concern, which I have ever had for your service, that it was not possible for you to carry on your government much longer, with so much partiality to one sort of men, though they lose no occasion of disserving you, and of showing the greatest inveteracy against my Lord Marlborough and my Lord Treasurer; and so much discouragement to others, who even after great disobligations, have taken several opportunities to show their firmness to your Majesty's interest, and their zeal to support you, and your ministers too, only because they had been faithful and useful servants to you and the public.

" This was all the sense and meaning of my letter, and if you can find fault with this, I am so unhappy as that you must always find fault with me, ' I am uncapable of thinking otherwise as long as I live, or of acting now but upon the same principle that I served you before you came to the crown for so many years, when your unlimited favour and kindness to me, could never tempt me to make use of it in one single instance that was not for your interest and service.' I am afraid I have been too long in explaining my thoughts upon the subject of my own letter, which it seems has been so great an offence, and how justly I leave you to judge; and I must beg your patience, since I am not very like to trouble you again, to let me say something upon the subject of your letter to my Lord Treasurer, which he has shewn me to day, with more concern than I know how to express : This was indeed the subject of my own letter, and the occasion of it, for I do not only see the uneasiness and the grief he has to leave your service, when you seem so desirous he should continue in it, but I see as well as he, the impossibility of his being able to support it, or himself, or my Lord Marlborough, for it all hangs upon one thread ; and when they are forced to leave your service, ' you will then indeed, find yourself in the hands of a violent party, who I am sure will have very little mercy or even humanity for you.' Whereas you might prevent all these misfortunes, by giving my Lord Treasurer and my Lord Marlborough (whom you may so safely trust) leave to propose those things to you, which they know and can judge to be absolutely necessary for your service, which will put it in their power to influence those, who have given you proofs both of their being able to serve you, and of their desiring to make you great and happy. But rather than your Majesty will employ a party-man, as you are pleased to call Lord Sunderland, you will put all things in confusion, and at the same time that you say this, you employ Sir C. Hedges, who is in one against you, only that he has voted in remarkable things that he might keep his place; and he did the same thing in the late King's time, till at last, that every body saw he was just dying and he could lose nothing by differing with that court: But formerly he voted with those men, the enemies to this government call whigs, and if he had not been a party-man, how could he have been a secretary of state, when all your councils were influenced by my Lord R. Lord Nott. Sir E. Seymour, and about six or seven more just such men, that call themselves *the heroes for the church ?* But what church can any man be of that would disturb so just a government as yours, or how can any body be in the true interest of England, that opposes you and your ministers, by whose advice, in four years' time, you are very near pulling down the power of France, and making *that religion, they only talk of, not only more secure than in any of the late reigns, but putting it upon a better foundation than it has been since the reformation. ?*"

" You are pleased to say you think it a great hardship, to persuade a man to part with a place he is in possession of, for one that is not vacant. In some cases that were certainly right, but not in this; for Sir Charles Hedges can have the place he desires immediately, and it is much better for him, unless he could be secretary of state for life. He will have two places that are considerable, one of which he can compass no other way, and this is so far from being a hardship, that he and all the world must think it a great kindness done him, and he must be a very weak man, if he lost the opportunity of having such a certainty, when he can't flatter himself that (whatever happens) he can be supported long in a place of that consequence for which he is so unfit. He has no capacity, no quality, no interest, nor ever could have been in that post, but that every body knows, my Lord Rochester cares for nothing so much as a man that he thinks will depend upon him. I beg your Majesty's pardon for not waiting upon you, and I persuade myself, that long as my letter is, it will be less troublesome to your Majesty."

It was a wonder to many, that this affair of my Lord Sunderland's promotion met with such difficulties, considering his relation to my Lord Marlborough, whose merit with his Queen and country was every year augmenting. For, whilst this matter was in suspence, he obtained the victory of Ramillies: on which occasion her Majesty, in a letter dated from Kensington, May 17, 1706, told him " ——She wanted words to express the true sense she had of the great service he had done his country and her, in that great and glorious victory, and hoped it would be a means to confirm all good and honest people in their principles, and frighten others from being troublesome ;——and then spoke, " of the allay it was to all her satisfaction, to consider what hazards he was exposed to,"——and repeated an obliging request she had often made, " that he would be careful of himself." I cannot doubt of the Queen's kind dispositions to my Lord Marlborough at this time, or her willingness, in general, to oblige him. And it quickly appeared that the difficulties raised by her Majesty against parting with Sir Charles Hedges, were wholly owing to the artifice and management of Mr. Harley, the other secretary of state, whose interest and secret transactions with the Queen were then doubtless in their beginning. This man had been put into that post by the Lords Marlborough and Godolphin when my Lord Nottingham in disgust resigned it. They thought him a very proper person to manage the House of Commons, upon which so much always depends: and his artifices had won upon them so far that they could not be persuaded, but they might securely trust him ; till experience too late convinced them of the contrary. And indeed (not to mention other parts of his behaviour) who would have thought that the man, who had wrote the following letter on occasion of Lord Blandford's death, could so soon have been laying schemes for the destruction of the person to whom it was written ?

" My Lord,—There is no servant of your Grace's is more sensibly affected with, I will not call it your Grace's loss, but our common misfortune, than myself. And I wish to God the part I can bear of it, would discharge your Grace of any of the burden. I do feel it, that a limb is torn off; therefore I think for the preservation of the residue, the blood should be staunched, I mean, grief should be moderated ; time I know is the best physician in this case, but our necessities require a quicker remedy. And I doubt not but your Grace's greatness of mind will give what is due to nature, without taking any thing from reason. Be pleased to consider that the nation are your children, the public needs all your care, how little soever it may deserve it.

"I shall pay my duty to your Grace, when you will permit me; in the mean time I beseech your pardon for this overflowing of my passion, which is the effect of the dutiful affection of,   " MY LORD,

"Your Grace's most humble and most obedient servant,

"*March* 1, 1703.   "Ro. HARLEY."

But to return, it is no wonder that Mr. Harley, with such views as he then had, should be unwilling to see a secretary of state displayed, over whom he thought he had some influence, and through whose hands the greater part of the business of his own office (scandalously neglected by himself) used to pass; and much more unwilling to have him succeeded by a person over whom he had no power whatsoever.

As for Sir Charles Hedges, when he found how backward the Queen was to dismiss him, he was so prudent as to make a greater advantage to himself by quitting his post, than he could have done by holding it. And in the winter of 1706 Lord Sunderland was appointed to succeed him.

But notwithstanding this point thus carried by the whigs, they were soon alarmed again by the Queen's choice of two high-church divines, to fill two vacant bishoprics. Several of the whigs were disposed to think themselves betrayed by the ministry: the truth was, that the Queen's inclination to the tories being now soothed by flatteries and insinuations of her private counsellors, had begun to make it irksome to her to consult with her ministers upon any promotions, either in the church or the state. The first artifice of those counsellors was, to instil into the Queen notions of the high prerogative of *acting without her ministers*, and, as they expressed it, of being *Queen indeed*. And the nomination of persons to bishoprics against the judgment and *remonstrances* of her ministry, being what they knew her genius would fall in with more readily than any thing else they could propose, they began with that; and they took care that those remonstrances should be interpreted by the world, and resented by herself as hard usage, a denial of common civility, and even *the making her no Queen*.

Her Majesty, however, to quiet the dissatisfaction of the whigs for the late promotions, ordered her ministers to assure them, that she would prefer no more tories, and she gave the same assurances with her own mouth in the cabinet council. And she was suffered by her secret counsellors so far to observe this promise, as to give, about the same time, the Bishopric of Norwich to Dr. Trimnel; a particular friend of Lord Sunderland. And she also, some time after, gave the Professorship of Divinity at Oxford to Dr. Potter, the present Archbishop of Canterbury, who had Dr. Smalridge for his competitor, recommended by the tories. But this latter favour to the whigs was not so easily obtained as the former. And upon the delays that were made in bestowing it, my Lord Marlborough thought it proper to try what credit he had with a Queen, whose glory he had carried to a height beyond that of any of her predecessors. He wrote therefore a very moving letter to her, complaining of the visible loss of his interest with her, and particularly of her so long deferring the promotion she had promised, of the person recommended by her ministry, as a faithful friend to her government, adding, that the only way to make her reign easy was to be true to that rule, which she had professed to lay down, of preferring none of those who appeared against her service and the nation's interest, &c.—He wrote at the same time, to the same effect, to me, and I wrote to the Queen, and at length, by much solicitation, this matter was obtained, and Dr. Potter fixed in the Professorship.

But this was only yielding up one small point, in order to conceal a much greater design and bring it to effect, when the season should be ripe for it. It was about this time, that the ministry began to be assured of the secret practices of Mr. Harley against them; and that I discovered the base returns made me by Mrs. Masham, upon whom I had heaped the greatest obligations.

The story of this Lady, as well as of *that Gentleman*, who was her great adviser and director, is worth the knowledge of posterity, as it will lead them into a sense of the instability of court-favour, and of the incurable baseness which some minds are capable of contracting.

Mrs. Masham was the daughter of one Hill, a merchant in the city, by a sister of my father. Our grandfather, Sir John Jenyns, had two and twenty children, by which means the estate of the family (which was reputed to be about 4000*l.* a year) came to be divided into small parcels. Mrs. Hill had only 500*l.* to her portion. Her husband lived very well, as I have been told, for many years, till turning projector, he brought ruin upon himself and his family. But as this was long before I was born, I never knew there were such people in the world, till after the Princess Anne was married, and when she lived at the Cockpit; at which time an acquaintance of mine came to me and said, *She believed I did not know, that I had relations who were in want*, and she gave me an account of them. When she had finished her story, I answered, *that indeed I had never heard before of any such relations*, and immediately gave her out of my purse ten guineas for their present relief, saying, I would do what I could for them. Afterwards I sent Mrs. Hill more money, and saw her. She told me that her husband was in the same relation to Mr. Harley, as she was to me, but that he had never done any thing for her.

I think Mrs. Masham's father and mother did not live long after this. They left four children, two sons and two daughters. The elder daughter (afterwards Mrs. Masham) was a grown woman. I took her to St. Albans, where she lived with me and my children, and I treated her with as great kindness, as if she had been my sister. After some time a bedchamber-woman of the Princess of Denmark's died; and as in that reign (after the Princesses were grown up) rockers, though not gentlewomen, had been advanced to be bedchamber-women, I thought I might ask the Princess to give the vacant place to Mrs. Hill. At first indeed I had some scruple about it, but this being removed by persons I thought wiser, with whom I consulted, I made the request to the Princess, and it was granted.

As for the younger daughter (who is still living) I engaged my Lord Marlborough, when the Duke of Gloucester's family was settled, to make her laundress to him, which was a good provision for her. And when the Duke of Gloucester died, I obtained for her a pension of 200*l.* a year, which I paid her out of the privy-purse. And in some time after I asked the Queen's leave to buy her an annuity out of some of the funds, representing to her Majesty, that as the privy-purse money produced no interest, it would be the same thing to her, if instead of the pension to Mrs. Hill, she gave her at once a sum sufficient to purchase an annuity; and that by this means her Majesty would make a *certain* provision for one, who had served the Duke of Gloucester. The Queen was pleased to allow the money for that purchase, and it is very probable that Mrs. Hill has the annuity to this day, and perhaps nothing else, unless she saved money after her sister had made her deputy to the privy-purse, which she did, as soon as she had supplanted me.

The elder son was, at my request, put by my Lord Godolphin into a place in the *custom-house*; and when, in order to his advancement to a better, it was necessary to give security for his good behaviour, I got a relation of the Duke of Marlborough's to be bound for him in two thousand pounds.

His brother (whom the bottle-men afterwards called *honest* Jack Hill) was a tall boy, whom I clothed (for he was all in rags), and put to school at St. Albans to one Mr. James, who had been an usher under Dr. Busby of Westminster. And whenever I went to St. Albans I sent for him, and was as kind to him as if he had been my own child. Afer he had learnt what he could there, a vacancy happening of page of honour to the Prince of Denmark, his Highness was pleased, at my request, to take him. I afterwards got my Lord Marlborough to make him groom of the bed-chamber to the Duke of Gloucester. And though my Lord always said that Jack Hill *was good for nothing*, yet to oblige me, he made him his *aid-de-camp*, and afterwards gave him a *regiment.* But it was his sister's interest that raised him to be a *general,* and to command in that ever memorable expedition to Quebec : I had no share in doing him these honours. To finish what I have to say upon his subject : When Mr. Harley thought it useful to attack the Duke of Marlborough in Parliament, this Quebec *general*, this *honest* Jack Hill, this *once ragged boy, whom I clothed,* happening to be sick in bed, was nevertheless persuaded by his *sister* to get up, wrap himself in warmer clothes than those I had given him, and go to the house to vote against the Duke.

I may here add, that even the *husband* of Mrs. Masham had several obligations to me. It was at my instance that he was first made a page, then a querry, and afterwards groom of the bed-chamber to the Prince; for all which he himself thanked me as for favours procured by my means.

As for Mrs. Masham herself, I had so much kindness for her, and had done so much to oblige her, without having ever done any thing to offend her, that it was too long before I could bring myself to think her other than a true friend, or forbear rejoicing at any instance of favour shown her by the Queen. I observed indeed at length that she was grown more shy of coming to me, and more reserved than usual, when she was with me ; but I imputed this to her peculiar moroseness of temper, and for some time made no other reflection upon it.

The first thing that led me into enquiries about her conduct, was, the being told (in the summer of 1707,) that my cousin Hill was privately married to Mr. Masham. I went to her and asked her if it were true, she owned it was, and begged my pardon for having concealed it from me. As much reason as I had to take ill this reserve in her behaviour, I was willing to impute it to bashfulness and want of breeding, rather than to any thing worse. I embraced her with my usual tenderness, and very heartily wished her joy; and then, turning the discourse, entered into her concerns in as friendly a manner as possible, contriving how to accommodate her with lodgings, by removing her sister into some of my own. I then enquired of her very kindly, whether the Queen knew of her marriage; and very innocently offered her my service, if she needed it, to make that matter easy. She had by this time learnt the art of dissimulation pretty well, and answered with an air of unconcernedness, that the *bed-chamber women had already acquainted the Queen with it,* hoping by this answer to divert any farther examination into the matter. But I went presently to the Queen and asked her, *why she had not been so kind as to tell me of my cousin's marriage,* expostulating with her upon the point, and putting her in mind of what she used often to say to me out of *Montaigne, That it was no breach* of promise of secrecy to tell such a friend any thing, because it was no *more than telling it to one's self.* All the answer I could obtain from her Majesty was this, *I have a hundred times bid Masham tell it you, and she would not.*

The conduct both of the Queen and of Mrs. Masham, convinced me that there was some mystery in the affair, and thereupon I set myself to enquire as particularly as I could into it. And in less than a week's time, I discovered, " that my cousin was become an absolute favourite; that the Queen herself was present at her marriage in Dr. Arbuthnot's lodgings," at which time her Majesty had called for a round sum out of the privy-purse; " that Mrs. Masham came often to the Queen, when the Prince was asleep, and was generally two hours every day in private with her :" And I likewise then discovered beyond all dispute " Mr. Harley's correspondence and interest at court by means of this woman."

I was struck with astonishment at such an instance of ingratitude, and should not have *believed,* if there had been any room left for *doubting.*

My Lord Marlborough was at first no less incredulous than I, as appears by the following paragraph of a letter from him, in answer to one from me on this subject.

" *Meldest, June 3d,* 1707.—The wisest thing is to have to do with as few people as possible. If you are sure that Mrs. Masham speaks of business to the Queen, I should think, you might with some caution tell her of it, which would do good. For she certainly must be grateful and will mind what you say."

It became easy now to decipher many particulars, which had hitherto remained mysterious, and my reflection quickly brought to my mind many passages, which had seemed odd and unaccountable, but had left no impression of suspicion or jealousy. Particularly I remembered that a long while before this, being with the Queen (to whom I had gone very privately by a secret passage, from my lodgings to the bedchamber), on a sudden this woman, not knowing that I was there, came in with the boldest and gaiest air possible, but, upon sight of me, stopped; and immediately, changing her manner, and making a most solemn courtesy, said, *did your Majesty ring ?* and then went out again. This singular behaviour needed no interpreter *now,* to make it understood. But not to dwell on such trifling incidents, as soon as I had got a thorough insight into her management, being naturally frank and open, I wrote to her the following letter.

" *Sept. 23d,* 1707.—Since the conversation I had with you at your lodgings, several things have happened to confirm me in what I was hard to believe, that you have made me returns very unsuitable to what I might have expected. I always speak my mind so plainly, that I should have told you so myself, if I had had the opportunity which I hoped for. But being now so near parting, think this way of letting you know it is like to be the least uneasy to you, as well as to ⠀⠀⠀⠀" Your humble servant,⠀⠀⠀⠀" S. MARLBOROUGH."

Though I was to go to Woodstock the next day, I staid at Windsor almost all the morning to wait her answer. But this could not be had so soon, it being necessary to consult with her great director in so nice a matter. At length, however, an answer was sent after me, the whole frame and style of which shewed it to be the genuine product of an artful man, who knew perfectly well the management of such an affair.

" *Windsor, Sept. 24th.* 1707.—While I was expecting a message from your Grace, to wait upon you according to your commands, last night, I received a letter which surprises me no less than it afflicts me, because it lays a most heavy charge upon me, of an ungrateful behaviour to your Grace. Her Majesty was pleased to tell me, that you was angry with me for not acquainting you with my marriage. I did believe after so generous a pardon, your Grace would think no more of that. I am very confident by the expression of your letter, that somebody has told some malicious lie of me to your Grace, from which it is impossible for me to vindicate myself till I know the crime I am accused of. I am sure, Madam, your goodness cannot deny me what the meanest may ask the greatest; I mean justice, to know my accuser. Without that, all friendship must be at the mercy of every malicious liar, as they are, who have so barbarously and unjustly brought me under your displeasure, the greatest unhappiness that could befal me; I therefore make it my most humble request to your Grace, that if ever I had the least share of your friendship, you would be pleased to give me that parting token to let me know who this wicked person is, and then I do not doubt but I shall make it plain how much they have wronged me, as well as imposed upon your Grace. As my affliction is very great, you will I hope in compassion let me hear from you, and believe me what I really am, "Madam,

"Your Grace's most humble and faithful servant, "A. HILL."

As I believe no body at this time doubts whether the writer of this letter was practising with the Queen to undermine me, I shall make no reflections upon it. My answer to it was in these terms,

"I received your letter upon the road to this place, and I can assure you the occasion of my complaints did not proceed from any ill offices that had been done you to me by any body, but from my own observation, which makes the impression much the stronger. But I think the subject is not very proper for a letter, and therefore I must defer it till we meet, and give you no farther trouble at this time from,

"Your most humble servant, "S. MARLBOROUGH."

About the same time that I made this discovery of Mrs. Masham's *intriguing*, my Lord Godolphin (as I before-mentioned), got notice of Mr. Harley's practices both within doors and without. He was endeavouring to create in the whigs jealousies of Lord Godolphin, and Lord Marlborough, and at the same time assuring the tories, that they might depend upon the Queen's inward affection to *them*; and that it was wholly owing to those two great Lords that the tories were not still possessed of all the places and employments. His design was to ruin the whigs, by disuniting them from the ministry, and so to pave the way for the tories to rise again; whom he thought to unite in himself, as their head, after he had made it impossible for them to think of a reconciliation with the Duke of Marlborough and Lord Godolphin.

But, that this able politician might in all things act suitably to his parts and genius, he, at the same time that he was employed in the manner I have related, was endeavouring to blind the eyes of those, whose destruction he aimed at, by most elaborate compliments, and the most nauseous professions of affection and duty.

I am persuaded, my Lord, that as mean an opinion as you have of this gentleman, you will yet be surprised at his manner of writing to my Lord Marlborough and myself. I have picked out of the letters we had from him, some choice pieces, which I think are real curiosities, and, when compared with his after conduct, will serve excellently well towards forming a perfect idea of his character.

"MADAM, Though the advantage the public receives from this great and glorious victory of Schellenberg is enough to inspire every one's heart with joy, who loves either the Queen or the nation, yet I must profess *I have a peculiar satisfaction;* it enhances the blessing to *me* by the hand that wrought it: I should have had a share in common with the rest of the nation, if another had performed it: But when the Duke of Marlborough is the author, when our deliverance, I may call it, is owing to *his* courage and *his* conduct; when the English honour is not only retrieved, but carried to so great a height, I cannot but receive an *additional pleasure* that it is *done by my Lord Duke.* I hope your Grace will forgive this overflowing of joy, as an instance of the sincerity and duty wherewith I shall always endeavour to distinguish myself,

"Madam, Your Grace's most humble and most obedient servant,

July 3, 1704.   "R. HARLEY."

"*May* 17, 1706.—MY LORD, Yesterday about seven in the evening. Col. Richards brought the most acceptable news of the glorious success your Grace had obtained in attacking the French army; and at the same time we are rejoicing for the victory, we cannot (I mean every good Englishman) but be sensibly touched with the danger all was in, by the hazard your Grace exposed your own person to, that deliverance enhances the value of the victory, considering how dear it had like to have cost us: heaven hath preserved that precious life, and would not suffer us to lose your Grace, who was born for the delivery of your own country, and the rescue of so many others from tyranny and oppression. Your Grace does not only triumph over the public enemies by teaching us how to conquer abroad, but you deliver us from ourselves, and rescue us from that tyranny which each party here would exercise upon one another: you have again disarmed malice, and though your glorious actions will encrease envy, yet the lustre of what you have done will discover it, and consequently render it impotent. May your Grace still go on prosperously, the best general, to the best Queen, and engaged in the best cause; and may you live long to enjoy in peace the fruits of your innumerable hazards and toils.

"I am with the greatest duty and affection,

"MY LORD, Your Grace's most humble, and most obedient servant,

"Ro. HARLEY."

"*May* 24, (*June* 4,) 1706.—MY LORD, I cannot tell where this letter will find your Grace, the improvements you make of your glorious victory are so stupendous; you have united the characters of Scipio and Hannibal; your Grace knows how to conquer, and how to improve a victory to admiration. Among the letters which have fallen into my hands, there is one to Mr. D'Allegre hath this article, that the Elector of Bavaria had wrote to his brother the Elector of Cologne, in these terms. *Avec la plus belle armée et la plus florissante et animée j'ay été battu, Dieu l'a voulu.* I hear from one I sent to Calais, that after the news of the victory and the declaring of Brussels, the mob of Calais were very troublesome in the town, and had your Grace's name continually in their mouths: we are assured that an express was sent away May 25, N. S. to Mr. Feuillade, to offer the Duke of Savoy any terms whatever. I doubt not but their emissaries will be busy also in Holland again, but I wrote last post to Mr. Buys, to caution him upon that subject, how necessary it was to be very vigilant, &c. I am with the greatest duty and affection,

"My Lord,

"Your Grace's most humble and most obedient servant,

"Ro. HARLEY."

"*May,* 28 *(June* 8*),* 1705.—MY LORD, I received this morning the honour of your Grace's letter of June 3, and cannot but observe, with the utmost pleasure and satisfaction, the great and wonderful successes which attend every day your Grace's prudent and most valiant conduct. It is very true, that victories have been obtained over potent and flourishing armies formerly. Your Grace gave us two years since a noble instance of that, but give me leave to say, this is not only obtaining a victory, but wearing of it too; this is improving your own actions, and outdoing your own victories, for nothing but you, Sir, can outdo my Lord Marlborough's former victories.

"Your proceedings are so swift that it is scarce possible with thought to keep pace with them; therefore we can only here give directions at random, &c.

" I am with the greatest duty and affection,

" My Lord, Your Grace's most humble and most obedient servant,

" Ro. HARLEY."

"*May* 31, *(June* 11,) 1706—.MY LORD, What success this fortunate raising of the siege (of Barcelona) will have upon the minds of the Portuguese I cannot tell, all sorts of people here are much exasperated against them; and Schonnenbergh now writes to his masters, that he suspects some of those ministers are in the interest of France: and I believe all of them hope for a civil war in Spain, of which they will make their markets. *But the glorious things your Grace has done, puts an end to such little projects. Your Grace does all at once, and the influence of it will be as extensive as the grandeur of the action,* &c.   I am with the greatest duty and affection,

" MY LORD, Your Grace's most humble and most obedient servant,

" Ro. HARLEY."

"*Thursday, Aug.* 8, 1706.—MADAM, I was just going to end this trouble, when I was honoured with your Grace's commands, which I shall apply myself to obey with all imaginable chearfulness and diligence. I cannot think of a servant and a spy, without the utmost abhorrence, and particularly when I find it levelled at *your Grace's family, to whom we all owe so much. I have been often provoked to see so much public and private ingratitude exercised towards the Duke.*

"I shall not omit any thing which may tend towards a discovery of this villainy; and I will not put it into any one's hands, but manage that myself. I beg your Grace will do me the honour to believe me to be, with the utmost duty,

"MADAM, Your Grace's most humble, and most obedient servant,

" Ro. HARLEY."

Is it not amazing, that a person, who could thus extol the Duke of Marlborough's services to his country, speak of his glory as beyond the power of envy or malice to hurt it, and profess so feel such *a peculiar joy* in the contemplation of it; is it not amazing, I say, that this very person should be, at the same time, contriving how to ruin that glorious man, in order to raise himself upon his ruins? The Duke was too backward to believe him capable of such designs, though it is certain he never had entertained the same good opinion of him, as my Lord Godolphin had, and though, as one may collect from a paragraph in a letter of Mr. Harley's, dated 25 March 1707, the Duke had been early warned of his practices. The paragraph contains these words.

" I return your Grace most hearty and humble thanks for the favourable expressions in your letter. I beg leave to assure you, that *I serve you by inclination and principle,* and a very little time will make that manifest, as well as that *I have no views or aims of my own.*

The conduct which Mr. Harley observed, after these assurances, was so directly contrary to them, and became quickly so notorious, that my Lord Godolphin could not help representing it to the Queen as of the utmost prejudice to her affairs: And when he found that her Majesty *would believe nothing of it,* he went so far as to say, that if Mr. Harley continued to act the part he did, and yet to have so much credit with her, as he perceived he had, Lord Marlborough and himself must of necessity quit her service. The Queen appeared pretty much alarmed at this, and presently wrote a letter to me, in which were several expressions of great kindness.

"*Kensington, Oct. the 30th.*—If I have not answered all my dear Mrs. Freeman's letters (as indeed I should have done), I beg she would not impute it to any thing but the apprehensions I was in of saying, what might add to the ill impressions she has of me. For though I believe we are both of the same opinion in the main, I have the misfortune that I cannot agree exactly in every thing, and therefore what I say is not thought to have the least colour of reason in it, which makes me really not care to enter into particulars ; but though I am unwilling to do it, it is impossible for me to help giving you some answer to your last letter, in which I find you think me insensible of every thing. I am very sorry, you, who have known me so long, can give way to such a thought, as that I do not think the parting with my Lord Marlborough and my Lord Treasurer of much consequence, because I did not mention any thing of my Lord Marlborough's kind letter concerning me. The reason of that was I really was in a great hurry when I writ to you, and not having time to write on that subject to both, I thought it was the most necessary to endeavour to let him see he had no reason to have suspicions, of any one's having power with me, besides himself and my Lord Treasurer, and I hope they will believe me.

"Can dear Mrs. Freeman think that I can be so stupid, as not to be sensible of the great services that my Lord Marlborough and my Lord Treasurer have done me, nor of the great misfortune it would be, if they should quit my service? No, sure, you cannot believe me to be so void of sense and gratitude. I never did, nor never will give them any just reason to forsake me ; and they have too much honour and too sincere a love for their country to leave me without a cause. And I beg you would not add that to my other misfortunes, of pushing them on to such an unjust and unjustifiable action. I think I had best say no more for fear of being too troublesome. But whatever becomes of me, I shall always preserve a most sincere and tender passion for my dear Mrs. Freeman to my last moment."

After my return to London, I had another kind letter from her Majesty in the following terms.

Saturday Night—"My dear Mrs. Freeman, I cannot go to bed without renewing a request that I have often made, that you would banish all unkind and unjust thoughts of your poor unfortunate, faithful Morley, which I saw by the glimpse I had of you yesterday you were full of. Indeed I do not deserve them, and if you could see my heart, you would find it as sincere, as tender, and passionately fond of you as ever, and *truly sensible of your kindness in telling me your mind upon all occasions.* Nothing shall ever alter me. Though we have the misfortune to differ in some things, I will ever be the same to my dear dear Mrs. Freeman, who I do assure once more, I am more tenderly and sincerely hers than it is possible ever to express."

I was every day in expectation of hearing from Mrs. Masham, who, I supposed, would now endeavour to clear up what had created so much uneasiness between us. But, to my great surprise, I was twelve days at St. James's under the same roof with her, before I had so much as any message from her. At length having one night past by her window in my return home, she sent one of her maids to my woman to ask *her* how I did, and to let me know that she was going to Kensington. This behaviour was so very ridiculous, that the next time I saw the Queen I could not forbear speaking of it, and at the same time telling her all that had past between us. The Queen looked grave and said, "she was mightily in the right not to come near me." I answered that I did not understand *that*, since she had expressed such a concern at my displeasure, and since the clearing up of matters had been reserved to our meeting. The Queen replied, that "it was very natural for her to be afraid to come to me, when she saw I was angry with her." To this I answered, that "she could have no reason to be afraid, unless she knew herself guilty of some crime." It was the Queen's usual way on any occasion, where she was predetermined (and my Lord Marlborough has told me that it was her father's) to repeat over and over some principal words she had resolved to use, and to stick firmly to them. She continued therefore to say, *it was very natural, and she was very much in the right.* So that this conversation with her Majesty produced nothing but an undeniable proof, that the new favourite was deeply rooted in her heart and affections; and that it was thought more advisable to let the breach between me and Mrs. Masham grow wider and wider, than to use any method to make it up.

But now within two days, Mrs. Masham contrived to make me a visit when I was abroad. Upon observing this, and considering that our meeting could be to no purpose but to draw fruitless and false professions from her, I gave a general order to my servants to say, whenever she should call, that I was not at home. After some time, it was thought proper that she should write to me, and desire I would see her; to which I consented, and appointed her a time. When she came, I began to tell her, *that it was very plain, that the Queen was much changed towards me, and that I could not attribute this to any thing but her secret management; that I knew she had been very frequently with her Majesty in private, and that the very attempt to conceal this, by artifice, from such a friend as I had been to her, was alone a very ill sign, and enough to prove a very bad purpose at bottom.* To this she answered, *that she was sure the Queen, who had loved me extremely, would always be very kind to me!* It was some minutes before I could recover from the surprise, with which so extraordinary an answer struck me. To see a woman whom I had raised out of the dust, put on such a superior air, and to hear her assure me, by way of consolation, *that the Queen would always be very kind to me!* At length I went on to reproach her with her ingratitude and her secret management with the Queen to undermine those, who had so long, and with so much honour served her Majesty. To this she answered, *that she never spoke to the Queen about business, but that she sometimes gave her petitions, which came to the back stairs, and with which she knew I did not care to be troubled.* And with such insincere answers she thought to colour over the matter, while I knew for certain, she had, before this, obtained pensions for several of her friends, and had frequently paid to others, out of the privy purse, sums of money, which the Queen had ordered me to bring her; and that she was, every day, long with her Majesty in private.

But thus our conversation ended, and when we had sat a while silent, she rose up and said, " she hoped I would give her leave to come sometimes and inquire after my health ;" which, however, it is plain, she did not design to do ; for she never once came near me after this. Notwithstanding which, when she owned her marriage publicly, I went with Lady Sunderland to visit her ; not that I intended to have any further intercourse with her, or to dissemble the ill opinion I had of her (as I had fully resolved to let her *then* know, in case I found an opportunity of speaking to her privately), but purely out of respect to the Queen, and to avoid any noise or disagreeable discourse, which my refusing that ordinary part of civility might occasion.

Not many days after this, I went to pay my respects to the Queen in the Christmas-holidays, and before I went in, I learnt from the page that Mrs. Masham was just then sent for. The moment I saw her Majesty, I plainly perceived she was very uneasy. She stood all the while I was with her, and looked as coldly upon me, as if her intention was, that I should no longer doubt of my loss of her affections. Upon observing what reception I had, I said, " I was very sorry I had happened to come so unseasonably." I was making my courtesy to go away, when the Queen, with a great deal of disorder in her face, and without speaking one word, took me by the hand : and when thereupon I stooped to kiss her's, she took me up with a very cold embrace, and then, without one kind word, let me go. So strange a treatment of me, after my long and faithful services, and after such repeated assurances from her Majesty of an unalterable affection, made me think that I ought, in justice to myself, as well as in regard to my mistress's interest, to write to her in the plainest and sincerest manner possible, and expostulate with her upon her change to me, and upon the new counsels, by which she seemed to be wholly governed. My letter was in these terms.

" *December the* 27*th,* 1707.—If Mrs. Morley will be so just as to reflect and examine impartially her last reception of Mrs. Freeman, how very different from what it has been formerly, when you were glad to see her come in, and sorry when she went away ; certainly you can't wonder at her reproaches, upon an embrace that seemed to have no satisfaction in it, but that of getting rid of her, in order to enjoy the conversation of one, that has the good fortune to please you much better, though I am sure no body did ever endeavour it with more sincerity than Mrs. Freeman has done. And if I had considered only my interest and that of my family, I might have borne this change without any complaint. For I believe Mrs. Morley would be sincere in doing us any good. But I have once been honoured with an open, kind confidence and trust, and that made all my service agreeable ; and it is not possible to lose it without a mortification too great to be passed in silence, being sure I have never done any thing to forfeit it, having never betrayed nor abused that confidence, by giving you a false representation of any body. My temper is naturally plain and sincere, and Mrs. Morley did like it for many years. It is not in the least altered. But I can't help thinking those things reasonable that appear to be so. And I appeal to God Almighty, that I never designed or pursued any thing, but as I was thoroughly convinced it was for Mrs. Morley's true interest and honour : and, I think, I may safely put it to that trial, if any thing has yet proved unsuccessful, that was of any public consequence, that Mrs. Freeman has been earnest to persuade Mrs. Morley to. And it is not possible for me to dissemble so as to appear what I am not.

" So much by way of apology for what happened upon Wednesday last. And if Mrs. Morley has any remains of the tenderness she once professed for her faithful Freeman, I would beg she might be treated oue of these two ways, either with the openness and confidence of a friend, as she was for twenty years ; (for to pretend kindness without trust and openness of heart is a treatment for children, not friends;) or else to that manner, that is necessary for the post she is in, which unavoidably forces her to be often troubling Mrs. Morley upon the account of others.   And if she pleases to chuse which of these ways, or any other she likes to have Mrs. Freeman live in, she promises to follow any rule that is laid down that is possible, and is resolved to her life's end, and upon all occasions to shew, that Mrs. Morley never had a more faithful servant."

My Lord Marlborough or my Lord Godolphin (I have forgot which) carried my letter.   The Queen took no notice of it to either of these Lords.   But some days after she wrote me an answer, in which she very much softened what had past.   I was much pleased to find her Majesty in that disposition; and once more put on as easy an appearance as I could.

But in a very short time after this, the great breach at court became public. Lord Marlborough and Lord Godolphin had often told the Queen in the most respectful manner, that it was impossible for them to do her any service, while Mr. Harley was in her confidence.   Her Majesty nevertheless seemed determined not to part with him ; till at length those two Lords, being urged by necessity to it, declared their resolution to serve no longer with him, and they absented themselves from the council.   Mr. Harley would have proceeded to business without them when the council met, but the Duke of Somerset said, he did not see how it could be to any purpose, when neither the General nor the Treasurer was present ; whereupon the council immediately broke up.   This had such an effect upon the Queen, that, very soon after, Mr. Harley was dismissed from his post.

Such a compliance with the ministers seemed to the world a very great concession, but was in truth nothing.   For it was evident by what followed, that this appearance of giving up Mr. Harley was with his own consent, and by his own advice, who, as long as Mrs. Masham continued in favour, would, under pretence of visiting her, (who was his cousin) have all the opportunities he could wish for, of practising upon the passions and credulity of the Queen ; and the method of corresponding with him had been settled some time before ; I was fully apprised of all this; yet I resolved to try, if by being easy and quiet I could regain any influence with her Majesty.   She had given me some encouragement to hope it.   For when, a little before Mr. Harley's dismission, Lord Marlborough resolved to quit the service, and when on that occasion I had with tears (which a tender concern at the thought of parting from her Majesty made me shed) represented to her, that if the Duke retired, it would be improper, and even impossible, for me to stay at court after him, she declared, " that she could not bear the thought of my leaving her, and that it must never be." And at that time she made me a promise that if ever I should leave her, (which, she again said, must never be) she would bestow my Offices among my children.

Nay, the whigs had some reason to flatter themselves about this time, that her Majesty would become better disposed to them, than she had hitherto been.

The Pretender's attempt to land in Scotland, which happened about this time, gave her an alarm, that seemed to bring a conviction along with it, that *the whigs were the most to be depended upon for the support of her government ; at least what she said in her answer to the Lords' address, upon the occasion, had this appearance. But as the danger presently blew over, and as her fears ceased with the cause of them, so all the hope which the whigs had raised in themselves from those fears, presently vanished.*

However, by the manner in which her Majesty wrote to the Duke of Marlborough, in a letter dated May 6th, 1708, she seems still to have retained a great degree of regard for *him*. After complaining to him of being so tired, that day, with importunities from whigs, that she had not spirits left to open her afflicted heart so freely and fully as she intended, she goes on to say, she is entirely of his opinion, thinking it neither for her honour nor interest to make steps (meaning the first steps) towards a peace, as the Duke had been pressed to do abroad; and assures him, that whatever insinuations her enemies might make to the contrary, she would never give her consent to a peace, but upon safe and honourable terms. She begs the Duke to be so just to her, as not to let the misrepresentations, made of her, have any weight with him: Adding, that it would be a greater trouble to her than could be expressed, and concludes with these words,—" I cannot end without begging you to be very careful of yourself, there being no body, I am sure, that prays more heartily than her, who will live and die most sincerely yours, &c."

The campaign of 1708 proved very glorious to the Duke of Marlborough by the victory at Oudenarde, the taking of Lisle, and the saving of Brussels. Her Majesty, on occasion of the victory, wrote the following letter to him.

" *Windsor, July the 6th,* 1708.—I want words to express the joy I have that you are well, after your glorious success; for which, next to God Almighty, my thanks are due to you. And indeed I can never say enough for all the great and faithful services you have ever done me. But be so just as to believe, I am as truly sensible of them as a grateful heart can be, and shall be ready to show it upon all occasions. I hope you cannot doubt of my esteem and friendship for you, nor think that because I differ with you in some things, it is for want of either: no, I do assure you. If you were here, I am sure you would not think me so much in the wrong in some things, as I fear you do now. I am afraid my letter should come too late to London, and therefore dare say no more, but that I pray God Almighty to continue his protection over you, and send you safe home again. And be assured I shall ever be sincerely your

" *Humble Servant.*"

To this the Duke answered.

" *July 23d,* 1708.—Madam,—I have the honour of your Majesty's letter of the 6th, and am very thankful for all your goodness to me. And I am sure it will always be my intention, as well as duty to be ready to venture my life for your service.

" As I have formerly told your Majesty that I am desirous to serve you in the army, but not as a minister, I am every day more and more confirmed in that opinion. And I think myself obliged upon all accounts, on this occasion, to speak my mind freely to you. The circumstances in this last battle, I think, shew the hand of God; for we were obliged not only to march five leagues that morning, but to pass a river before the enemy, and to engage them before the whole army was passed, which was a visible mark of the favour of heaven to you and your arms.

" Your Majesty shall be convinced from this time, that I have no ambition, or any thing to ask for myself or family. But I will end the few years which

I have to live in endeavouring to serve you, and to give God Almighty thanks for his infinite goodness to me. But as I have taken this resolution to myself, give me leave to say, that I think you are obliged in conscience, and as a good Christian, to forgive, and to have no more resentments to any particular person or party, but to make use of such as will carry on this just war with vigour; which is the only way to preserve our religion and liberties, and the crown on your head. Which that you may long enjoy, and be a blessing to your people, shall be the constant wish and prayer of him, that is with the greatest truth and duty,   " Madam, &c."

But now, what was very strange, the successes of my Lord Marlborough this year seemed rather to lower his credit with her Majesty, than to raise it; a thing so extremely out of the common course of nature, that no one, I think, can doubt of it's being the pure effect of art, the product of that wonderful talent Mr. Harley possessed, in the supreme degree, of confounding the common sense of mankind.

The Duke was perfectly sensible of the change in her Majesty towards him, and having complained of it in a letter to me, I sent this letter to her, inclosed in the following one from myself.

" I cannot help sending your Majesty this letter, to shew how exactly Lord Marlborough agrees with me in my opinion, that he has now no interest with you: Though when I said so in the church on Thursday (19th Aug. 1708.), you were pleased to say it was untrue. And yet I think he will be surprised to hear that when I had taken so much pains to put your jewels in a way that I thought you would like, Mrs. Masham could make you refuse to wear them, in so unkind a manner; because that was a power she had not thought fit to exercise before. I will make no reflections upon it; only that I must needs observe, that your Majesty chose a very wrong day to mortify me, when you were just going to return thanks for a victory obtained by Lord Marlborough."

In answer to this, her Majesty was pleased to write to me these few words.

" Sunday.—After the commands you gave me on the thanksgiving day of not answering you, I should not have troubled you with these lines, but to return the Duke of Marlborough's letter safe into your hands, and for the same reason do not say any thing to that, nor to yours which enclosed it."

Upon receiving so extraordinary a letter, I could not avoid writing again as follows.

" I shall not trouble your Majesty with any answer to your last short letter but to explain what you seem to mistake in what I said at church. I desired you not to answer me there for fear of being overheard. And this you interpret as if I had desired you not to answer me at all, which was far from my intention. For the whole end of my writing to you so often, was to get your answer to several things in which we differed, that if I was in the wrong, you might convince me of it, and I should very readily have owned my mistakes. But since you have not been pleased to show them to me, I flatter myself that, I have said several things to you that are unanswerable. And I hope some time or other you will find leisure to reflect upon them, and will convince Lord Marlborough, that he is mistaken in thinking that he has no credit with you, by hearkening sometimes to his advice; and then I hope you will never more be troubled with disagreeable letters from me: for I should be much better pleased to say and do every thing you like. But I should think myself wanting in my duty to your Majesty, if I saw you so much in the wrong, as without prejudice or passion, I really think you are in several particulars I have mentioned, and did not tell you of it. And the rather, because nobody else cares to speak out upon so ungrateful a subject. The word *command*, which you use at the beginning of your letter, is very unfitly supposed to come from me. For though I have always writ to you as a friend, and lived with you as such for so many years with all the truth and honesty and zeal for your service that was possible, yet I shall never forget that I am your subject, nor cease to be a faithful one."

Through the whole summer after Mr. Harley's dismission, the Queen continued to have secret correspondence with him. And that this might be the better managed, she staid all the sultry season, even when the Prince was panting for breath, in that small house, she had formerly purchased at Windsor, which, though as hot as an oven, was then said to be cool, because from the park such persons, as Mrs. Masham had a mind to bring to her Majesty, could be let in privately by the garden.

And when upon the death of the Prince, one would have thought that her Majesty's real grief would have made her avoid every place and every object that might sensibly revive the remembrance of her loss, she chose for her place of retirement his closet, and for some weeks, spent many hours in it every day. I was amazed at this; and when I spoke to her of it, she seemed surprised, just like a person who on a sudden becomes sensible of her having done something she would not have done, had she duly considered. But the true reason of her Majesty's chusing this closet to sit in, was that the back-stairs belonging to it came from Mrs. Masham's lodgings, who by that means could secretly bring to her whom she pleased.

And that a correspondence was thus carried on with Mr. Harley, became every day more and more manifest by the difficulties and objections which her Majesty had learnt to raise against almost every thing proposed by her ministers. Nay, it is well known, that Mr. Harley and his associates, when at length they had compassed their designs, and got into the management of affairs, did often (both in their cups and out of them) boast that they, while the Queen's ministers were asleep, were frequently at court giving advice in secret, how to perplex them in all their measures.

But they were much mistaken, if they imagined that their proceedings at the time I am speaking of, were so entirely covered. The ministers were fully convinced of the truth, and frequently represented to her Majesty, what a discouragement it was to them in their endeavours for her service, to find that she had no confidence in them, but was influenced by the counsel of others who counterworked them in every instance. Upon this subject, I myself wrote and spoke a great deal to her with my usual plainness and zeal. But finding, not only that I could make no impression on her in this respect, but that her change towards *me* in particular was every day more and more apparent, I at length went to her, and begged to know what my crime was, that had wrought in her so great an alteration. This drew from the Queen a letter, dated October 26, 1709, wherein she charges me "with inveteracy," as her word is "against poor Masham," and "with having nothing so much at heart as the ruin of my cousin." In speaking of the misunderstandings betwixt her Majesty and me, she says, they are "for nothing that she knows of, but because she cannot see with my eyes, and hear with my ears." And adds, "that it is impossible for me to recover her former kindness, but that she shall behave herself to me, as the Duke of Marlborough's wife, and her groom of the stole." This declaration so plain and express of her Majesty's thorough change towards me was the more extraordinary, as in this same letter are these words,

" you have asked me once or twice if you had committed any fault that I was so changed, and I told you, no; because I do not think it a crime in any one not to be of my mind."

Upon receipt of this letter, I immediately set myself to draw up a long narrative of a series of faithful services for about 26 years past; of the great sense the Queen formerly had of my services; of the great favour I had been honoured with on account of them; of the use I had made of that favour and of my losing it now by the artifice of my enemies, and particularly of one, whom I had raised out of the dust. And knowing how great a respect her Majesty had for the writings of certain eminent divines, I added to my narrative, the directions given by the author of the *whole duty of man* with relation to friendship; the directions in the *common prayer book* before the communion with regard to reconciliation, together with the rules laid down by Bishop Taylor upon the same head; and I concluded with giving my word to her Majesty, that if after reading these, she would please only to answer in two words, that she was still of the same opinion, as when she wrote that harsh letter, which occasioned her this trouble, I would never more give her the least trouble upon any subject, but the business of my office, as long as I should have the honour to continue her servant: assuring her, that however she might be changed towards me, and how much soever we might still differ in opinion, I should ever remember that she was my Mistress and my Queen, and should always pay her the respect due from a faithful servant and dutiful subject.

I sent from St. Albans this narrative, which she promised to read and answer. And ten days after, writing to me upon another occasion, she said she had not leisure yet to read all my papers, but when she had, she would send me some answer. But none ever came: nor had my papers any apparent effect on her Majesty, except that, after my coming to town, as she was passing by me, in order to receive the communion, she looked with much good nature and very graciously smiled upon me. But the smile and pleasant look I had reason afterwards to think were given to Bishop Taylor and the *common prayer book*, and not to me.

In the beginning of January 1709-10 the Earl of Essex died; and the Queen presently wrote to the Duke of Marlborough to give his regiment to Mr. Hill, a man who had been basely ungrateful to me who raised him; and whose sister, Mrs. Masham, the Duke well knew was at this time undermining the interest of himself, his family and friends.

The scheme of the Queen's new counsellors to make her ministers quit her service, or engage her to discard them, began now to appear without disguise. They durst not tell her Majesty at once all they designed, but, proposing to her only one thing at a time, led her by insensible degrees to the accomplishment of the whole. They began, as I before observed, with engaging her to nominate persons to bishoprics without consulting her ministers. And now they prevailed with her to appoint military officers, without advising with her general. And nothing could be more to their purpose, than this choice of Mr. Hill for Lord Essex's regiment, because they knew that nothing could be more disagreeable to the Duke of Marlborough, or would tend more to lessen his weight and authority in the army, and consequently at home too. The new counsellors saw that if the Duke readily yielded in this matter, it would sow discontent among the officers, and that a door would be opened for his enemies to come into the army and insult him. And on the other hand, if the Duke should not comply, or should show any reluctance in complying, this would furnish an excellent pretence for grievous complaints and outcries, *that the Queen was but a cypher and could do nothing.* It was indeed by representing her to herself, as a slave to the Marlborough family, that they worked upon her passions; while at the same time (as is too evident) they meant to make her in reality *their* slave, to do for them those drudgeries that would dishonour her, instead of following the counsels of ministers, whose fidelity she had experienced, and who had carried her glory to the highest pitch.

Upon this message from the Queen, the Duke waited upon her, and with all humility represented to her, what a prejudice it would be to her service, to have so young an officer preferred before so many others of higher rank and longer service. Besides, that the shewing so extraordinary and partial favour to Mrs. Masham's brother, could be interpreted no otherwise than as a declaring against all those who had so much reason to be uneasy with her; and that indeed it would be setting up a banner for all the discontented persons in the army to repair to. In short the Duke said every thing he could think of, and with all the moving concern that the nature of the affair created in him, to engage her Majesty to change her resolution. But all seemed to no purpose. He could not draw one kind expression from her, nor obtain any answer, but *that he would do well to advise with his friends.*

Lord Godolphin spoke often to her upon the same subject, representing to her the Duke's long, great, and faithful services, and the very bad influence which her intended favour to Mr. Hill must necessarily have in the army. But neither had this so much effect as to engage her to say one favourable word about the Duke. On the 15th of January therefore he left the town and went to Windsor in great discontent. It was council-day. The Queen did not ask where he was, nor take the least notice of his absence. His withdrawing himself made a great noise in the town. Many of the nobility spoke with earnestness to the Queen of the very ill consequences of mortifying a man, who had done her so long and important services. Her Majesty answered, that his services were still fresh in her memory, and that she had as much kindness for him as ever she had. The noise however still continued and increased, and there was a great discourse, not without probability, that some notice would be taken of the matter in the House of Commons, and some votes past disagreeable to her Majesty and her new counsellors. This design was laid to my charge, but I said enough to the Queen to vindicate myself from it. And it was indeed owing to the Duke's particular friends in the House, that no such notice was taken.

The new counsellors being alarmed with apprehensions of what the Parliament might do, and believing that they should be able at a proper season to make better use of the Queen's yielding up the point, than of her insisting upon it, gave her advice accordingly: so that January the 20th, she ordered Lord Godolphin to write to the Duke, *that he might dispose of the regiment as he himself thought fit:* and to desire him to come to town. But before this reached Lord Marlborough, he had written the following letter to the Queen.

"MADAM,—By what I heard from London, I find your Majesty is pleased to think, that when I have reflected, I must be of opinion, that you are in the right in giving Mr. Hill the Earl of Essex's regiment. I beg your Majesty will be so just to me, as not to think I can be so unreasonable, as to be mortified to the degree that I am, if it proceeded only from this one thing; for I shall always be ready and glad to do every thing that is agreeable to you, after I have represented what may be a prejudice to your service.   But this is only one of a great many mortifications, that I have met with.   And as I may not have many opportunities of writing to you, let me beg your Majesty to reflect what your own people, and the rest of the world must think, who have been witnesses of the love, zeal and duty, with which I have served you, when they shall see that after all I have done, it has not been able to protect me against the malice of a bed-chamber woman.   Your Majesty will allow me on this occasion to re-mind you of what I writ to you the last campaign, of the certain knowledge I had of Mrs. Masham's having assured Mr. Harley, that I should receive such constant mortifications, as should make it impossible for me to continue in your service.   God Almighty and the whole world are my witnesses, with what care and pains I have served you for more than twenty years, and I was resolved, if possible, to have struggled with the difficulties to the end of this war.   But the many instances I have had of your Majesty's great change to me, has so broke my spirits, that I must beg as the greatest and last favour, that you will approve of my retiring, so that I may employ the little time I have to live, in making my just acknowledgements to God, for the protection he has been pleased to give me.   And your Majesty may be assured that my zeal for you and my country is so great, that in my retirement I shall daily pray for your prosperity, and that those, who shall serve you as faithfully as I have done, may never feel the hard return that I have met with."

The Queen wrote him an answer, expressing some concern at several parts of his letter, assuring him, without entering into particulars, that he had no ground for suspicions, and desiring him to come to town.

But fearing at the same time that some motion might be made in Parliament against Mrs. Masham, which might be attended with very disagreeable consequences, she sent about in much concern, to many persons to stand by her, as if some great attack were going to be made upon her.   This application and the closetting some persons, who were known enemies to the Revolution, gave encouragement to the jacobites; several of whom were now observed running to court with faces full of business and satisfaction, as if they were going to get the Government into their hands.   And this being represented to the Queen, as a kind of victory gained by her over the Marlborough family, was doubtless one means of hindering all thoughts of a real accommodation.

In about a month after this, both Houses of Parliament addressed the Queen to order the Duke of Marlborough over into Holland, to attend to the great affair of a peace, (towards which there were then some overtures) and in case that project did not take effect, to prepare for an early opening the campaign.

The Queen in her answer to that address used these words.—" I am very glad to find by this address, that you concur with me in a just sense of the Duke of Marlborough's eminent services."

But notwithstanding this, he had not been long gone, before her Majesty gave a signal proof how much his declared enemies were in her favour, by granting Mr. Hill a pension of 1000 l. a year.   (And in some time, she made both him and Mr. Masham (men of little or no service) general officers, over the heads of many brave men, who had frequently hazarded their lives in her service, and had gone through the toils and hardships of a tedious war.)

In the mean time, as to myself, I learnt that the Queen was made to believe that I often spoke of her in company disrespectfully.   And I know myself wholly free from the guilt of this charge, and indeed incapable of it, I waited on her Majesty the 3d of April 1710, and begged of her that she would be pleased to give me a private hour, because I had something which I was very desirous of saying to her Majesty, before I went out of town. I named three several hours, in which I knew the Queen used to be alone, but she refused them all, in a very unusual and surprising manner: and at last she herself appointed six o'clock the next day, the hour of prayers, when she could least of all expect to be at leisure for any particular conversation. But even this small favour, though promised, was not thought advisable to be granted by her new counsellors. For, that night, she wrote a letter to me, in which she desired me "to lay before her in writing whatever I had to say, and to gratify myself by going into the country as soon as I could." I took the first opportunity of waiting upon the Queen again, and used all the arguments I could to obtain a private audience; alledging, that when her Majesty should hear what I had to say, she would herself perceive it impossible to put things of that nature into writing; that I was now going out of town for a great while, and perhaps should never have occasion to give her a like trouble as long as I lived. The Queen refused it several times in a manner hard to be described, but at last appointed the next day after dinner. Yet upon farther consideration it was thought advisable to break this appointment: for, the next morning she wrote to me to let me know, "that she should dine at Kensington, and that she once more desired me to put my thoughts into writing."

To this I wrote an answer, begging that her Majesty would give me leave to follow her to Kensington; and, that she might not apprehend a greater trouble than she would receive, I assured her Majesty, that what I had to say would not create any dispute or uneasiness, (it relating only to the clearing myself from some things which, I had heard, had very wrongfully been laid to my charge,) and could have no consequence, either in obliging her Majesty to answer, or to see me oftner than would be easy to her: adding, that if that afternoon were not convenient, I would come every day and wait till her Majesty would please to allow me to speak to her. Upon the sixth of April I followed this letter to Kensington, and by that means prevented the Queen's writing again to me, as she was preparing to do. The page who went in to acquaint the Queen that I was come to wait upon her Majesty staid longer than usual; long enough, it is to be supposed, to give time to deliberate whether the favour of admission should be granted, and to settle the measures of behaviour if I were admitted. But at last he came out, and told me I might go in. As I was entering the Queen said she was just going to write to me. And when I began to speak she interrupted me four or five times with these repeated words, "whatever you have to say, you may put it in writing." I said, her Majesty never did so hard a thing to any, as to refuse to hear them speak, and assured her, that I was not going to trouble her upon the subject which I knew to be ungrateful to her, but that I could not possibly rest till I had cleared myself from some particular calumnies with which I had been loaded. I then went on to speak, (though the Queen turned away her face from me,) and to represent my hard case: that there were those about her Majesty, who had made her believe that I had said things of her, which I was no more capable of saying than of killing my own children; that I seldom named her Majesty in company, and never without respect, and the like. The Queen said, "Without doubt there were many lies told." I then begged, in order to make this trouble the shorter, and my own innocence the plainer, that I might know the particulars of which I had been accused. Because, if I were guilty, that would quickly appear; and if I were innocent, this method only would clear me.   The Queen replied, " that she would give me no answer," laying hold on a word in my letter, that what I had to say in my vindication, " would have no consequence in obliging her Majesty to answer," &c. which surely did not at all imply, that I did not desire to know the particular things laid to my charge, without which it was impossible for me to clear myself. This I assured her Majesty was all I desired, and that " I did not ask the names of the authors or relators of those calumnies," saying all that I could think reasonable, to enforce my just request.   But the Queen repeated again and again the words she had used, without ever receding.   And it is possible that this conversation had never been consented to, but that her Majesty had been carefully provided with those words, as a shield to defend her against every reason I could offer.   I protested to her Majesty, that I had no design in giving her this trouble, to solicit the return of her favour, but that my sole view was to clear myself; which was too just a design to be disappointed by her Majesty. Upon this, the Queen offered to go out of the room, I following her, and begging leave to clear my self; and the Queen repeating over and over again, " You desired no answer, and shall have none."   When she came to the door, I fell into great disorder; streams of tears flowed down against my will, and prevented my speaking for some time.   At length I recovered myself, and appealed to the Queen, in the vehemence of my concern, whether I might not still have been happy in her Majesty's favour, if I could have contradicted or dissembled my real opinion of men, or things? whether I had ever, during our long friendship, told her one lie, or played the hypocrite once? whether I had offended in any thing, unless in a very zealous pressing upon her, that which I thought necessary for her service and security? I then said I was informed by a very reasonable and credible person about the court, that things were laid to my charge of which I was wholly incapable; that this person knew that such stories were perpetually told to her Majesty to incense her, and had begged of me to come and vindicate myself; that the same person had thought me of late guilty of some omissions towards her Majesty, being entirely ignorant how uneasy to her my frequent attendance must be, after what had happened between us.   I explained some things which I had heard her Majesty had taken amiss of me, and then with a fresh flood of tears, and a concern sufficient to move compassion, even where all love was absent, I begged to know what other particulars she had heard of me, that I might not be denied all power of justifying myself.   But still the only return was, " You desired no answer, and you shall have none."   I then begged to know if her Majesty would tell me some other time?—" You desired no answer, and you shall have none."   I then appealed to her Majesty again, if she did not herself know that I had often despised interest in comparison of serving her faithfully and doing right? And whether she did not know me to be of a temper incapable of disowning any thing which I knew to be true?—" You desired no answer, and you shall have none."   This usage was so severe, and these words, so often repeated, were so shocking (being an utter denial of common justice to one who had been a most faithful servant, and now asked nothing more) that I could not conquer myself, but said the most disrespectful thing I ever spoke to the Queen in my life, and yet, what such an occasion and such circumstances might well excuse, if not justify.   And that was, that " I was confident her Majesty would suffer for such an act of inhumanity."   The Queen answered, " that will be to myself."   Thus ended this remarkable conversation, the last I ever had with her Majesty. I shall make no comment upon it. The Queen always meant well, how much soever she might be blinded or misguided. But in a letter, which I had from the Duke of Marlborough, about eight months before, there is something so pertinent to the present occasion, that I cannot forbear transcribing the passage.

Aug. 26, 1709.————"It has always been my observation in disputes, especially in that of kindness and friendship, that all reproaches, though ever so just, serve to no end but making the breach wider. I cannot help being of opinion, that however insignificant we may be, there is a power above, that puts a period to our happiness or unhappiness. If any body had told me, eight years ago, that after such great success, and after you had been a faithful servant 27 years, that even in the Queen's life time, we should be obliged to seek happiness in a retired life, I could not have believed that possible."

I never saw the Queen after the interview I have been speaking of, nor ever had any correspondence with her, except on two occasions relating to the public, one of which I shall now mention, because it was the very next day after our parting. I received a letter from Lord Marlborough, with one enclosed to Lord Godolphin, who was then at New-market, and whose letters, at such times, and when dispatch was required, I had the privilege to open. In this letter the Duke gave Lord Godolphin an account of a man then coming to England, who, as Prince Eugene informed him, had been guilty of many vile practices at Vienna, and was a very great villain, desiring that he might not be admitted to see the Queen, but be immediately sent out of England. Hereupon I wrote a letter to her Majesty, in which, after saying that I thought it my duty to impart to her without delay what so nearly concerned her, I added, that I could not forbear taking notice of the usage I had met with, the day before, when I waited upon her; and when my only business was to be heard on a point that touched me very sensibly, in order to clear myself from what had been laid to my charge if I were innocent; or to beg pardon, if in any thing I had done amiss.

All the answer I received to this letter was in these few words, dated from Kensington.

"I received yours, with one enclosed from the D. of M. to Lord Treasurer, just as I was coming down stairs from St. James's, so could not return the enclosed back, till I came to this place."

But notwithstanding this thorough alienation of the Queen's affections from me, I was not yet divested of my employments. Perhaps it was not yet determined who should succeed me, nor whether it were proper, that Lord Marlborough should have that mortification, before the season was fully ripe for the execution of the new scheme. Matters had been greatly advanced towards maturity by the business of Sacheverel, which had engaged the attention of the nation for the greater part of the last winter. Every body knows that whole story, and the terrible cry that was raised about the danger of the church, from the attempt that was made in a Parliamentary way, to punish an ignorant, impudent incendiary, a man who was the scorn even of those who made use of him as a tool. I shall only observe, that the Duke of Shrewsbury, who had voted for the acquittal of that scurrilous declaimer against the Queen's ministers, was, in about three weeks after, appointed Lord Chamberlain by her Majesty.

When the Queen had resolved to make this step, she thought fit to write to my Lord Godolphin, then at New-market, to acquaint him with her resolution, and that she hoped she should have his approbation in this and all her actions.   The answer which he returned to her Majesty is so great a proof of his honest heart and clear understanding, and of the injustice of those whigs, who did not scruple to call in question his zeal and even his sincerity in their cause, that I think it is but discharging a debt I owe to his memory, to give a copy of his letter.

"*New-market, April 15th,* 1710.—I have the honour of your Majesty's letter of the 13th, by which I have the grief to find that what you are pleased to call spleen in my former letter, was only a true impulse and conviction of mind, that your Majesty is suffering yourself to be guided to your own ruin and destruction as fast as it is possible for them to compass it, to whom you seem so much to hearken.

" I am not therefore so much surprised, as concerned at the resolution which your Majesty says you have taken, of bringing in the Duke of Shrewsbury. For when people began to be sensible it would be difficult to persuade your Majesty to dissolve a Parliament, which for two winters together, had given you above six millions a year for the support of a war, upon which your crown depends; even while that war is still subsisting, they have had the cunning to contrive this proposal to your Majesty, which in its consequence will certainly put you under a necessity of breaking the Parliament, though contrary (I yet believe) to your mind and intention.

" I beg your Majesty to be persuaded, I do not say this out of the least prejudice to the Duke of Shrewsbury. There is no man of whose capacity I have had a better impression, nor with whom I have lived more easily and freely for above twenty years.   Your Majesty may please to remember, that at your first coming to the crown, I was desirous he should have had one of the chief posts in your service; and it would have been happy for your Majesty and the kingdom, if he had accepted that offer: But he thought fit to decline it, and the reasons generally given at that time for his doing so, do not much recommend him to your Majesty's service.   But I must endeavour to let your Majesty see things as they really are.   And to bring him into your service and into your business at this time, just after his being in a public open conjunction in every vote with the whole body of the tories, and in a private, constant correspondence and caballing with Mr. Harley in every thing, what consequence can this possibly have, but to make every man that is now in your cabinet council except   to run from it as they would from the plague.   And I leave it to your Majesty to judge, what effect this entire change of your ministers will have among your allies abroad, and how well this war is like to be carried on, in their opinion, by those who have all along opposed and obstructed it, and who will like any peace the better, the more it leaves France at liberty, to take their time of imposing the Pretender upon this country.

" These considerations must certainly make Holland run immediately into a separate peace with France, and make your Majesty lose all the honour, and all the reputation your arms had acquired by the war; and make the kingdom lose all the fruits of that vast expence which they have been at in this war, as well as all the advantage and safety which they had so much need of, and had so fair a prospect of obtaining by it.   And can any body imagine that after so great a disappointment to the kingdom, there will not be an enquiry into the causes of it; and who have been the occasion of so great a change in your Majesty's measures and counsels, which had been so long successful, and gotten you so great a name in the world? I am very much afraid your Majesty will find, when it is too late, that it will be a pretty difficult task for any body to stand against such an enquiry. I am sure if I did not think all these consequences inevitable, I would never give your Majesty the trouble and uneasiness of laying them before you. But, persuaded as I am that your Majesty will find them so, it is my indispensable duty to do it out of pure faithfulness and zeal for your Majesty's service and honour. Your Majesty's having taken a resolution of so much consequence to all your affairs both at home and abroad, without acquainting the Duke of Marlborough or me with it, till after you had taken it, is the least part of my mortification in this whole affair. Though perhaps the world may think the long and faithful services we have constantly and zealously endeavoured to do your Majesty, might have deserved a little more consideration. However for my own part, I most humbly beg leave to assure your Majesty, I will never give the least obstruction to your measures, or to any ministers you shall please to employ. And I must beg further, to make two humble requests to your Majesty, the one, that you will allow me to pass the remainder of my life always out of London, where I may find most ease and quiet. The other, that you would keep this letter and read it again about next Christmas, and then be pleased to make your own judgment, who hath given you the best and most faithful advice,   "I am," &c.

I think it is pretty plain from the Queen's letter, to which, what I have just now given was an answer, that her new counsellors did not open their whole scheme to her at once. For if they had, they certainly could never have engaged her to tell my Lord Godolphin that *she hoped he would approve of all her actions.* But they judged wisely, that passing on under their direction from one step to another, she would quickly come to a desperate necessity of going as far as they themselves wished.

About the beginning of June, the design of turning out Lord Sunderland began to be talked of. Lord Marlborough was now abroad at the head of the army.

As soon as the news of this design reached him, he wrote a very moving letter to the Queen, representing the very ill consequences it would necessarily have upon all affairs abroad, to have his son-in-law, against whose fidelity nothing could be objected, and in whom the allies had so entire a confidence, turned out of her service in the middle of a campaign; and begging it as a reward of all his past services, that she would at least delay her resolution till the campaign was ended. I was likewise urged by some friends to try to say something to divert if possible such a stroke; because it was given out that the Queen would do this chiefly on my account, that I might feel the effects of her displeasure in so sensible and tender a point. No consideration proper to myself, could have induced me to trouble the Queen again, after our last conversation. But I was overcome by the consideration of Lord Marlborough, Lord Sunderland and the public interest, and wrote in the best manner I could to the Queen June 7th, 1710, begging, for Lord Marlborough's sake, that she would not give him such a blow, of which I dreaded the consequence, putting her in mind of her letter about the Duke upon the victory at Blenheim; and adding, the most solemn assurances, that I had not so much as a wish to remove Mrs. Masham, and that all the noise which had been about an address for that purpose, had been occasioned by Lord Marlborough's discontents at that time which most people thought were just. To this the Queen wrote a very short and harsh answer, complaining that I had broke my promise of not saying any thing of politics, or of Mrs. Masham; and concluding, that it was plain from this ill usage what she was to expect for the future.

I could not forbear, for my own vindication, to write a second letter, in which I assured her Majesty, that I should not have troubled her with the first, but I heard it reported, that the persecution, begun against Lord Marlborough and his family, was chiefly occasioned by her Majesty's displeasure and aversion to me, as having promoted an address against Mrs. Masham; that it was only to vindicate myself from that aspersion, that I had presumed to trouble her; that I could not imagine it could be interpreted as an offence, to vindicate myself from what was now made the pretence for turning out Lord Sunderland, and pushing Lord Marlborough to extremities; that I had no reason to think, that the assuring her Majesty, that I would never have any hand in any thing against Mrs. Masham, could have been construed as an ungrateful speaking about her, or called a continuation of ill usage; that I thought this was rather a complying with her Majesty's inclination, and saying what she could not but approve; that all the politics in my letter was my concern for Lord Marlborough; making it at last my most earnest request, that her Majesty would only defer the blow till the end of the campaign. This, I added, I begged upon my knees, and left her Majesty to judge whether, after such an expression, it was likely that I should ever enter into any thing that could displease her.

Whether my interfering in this matter hastened the execution of the design, I cannot say   Certain it is that it did not retard it, for Lord Sunderland was presently after dismissed from his office.   On which occasion several great men, who wished well to their country, and who feared that my Lord Marlborough might in disgust quit the service, immediately wrote him a joint letter, which I shall here insert, in honour both of them and the Duke.

"*June 14th,* 1710.—My Lord, We should not have given your Grace the trouble of this joint letter, but for the great concern and uneasiness in which we find you, on account of my Lord Sunderland, by your letter of the 20th to my Lord Treasurer, which he has communicated to us.   That letter, as moving and as reasonable as it was, has not hindered the seals from being taken this morning from my Lord Sunderland.   No wonder then if the utmost endeavours which could be used to prevent it, and the strong arguments which have been made of the ill consequences, that must attend such steps both at home and abroad have met with so little success.   We find ourselves so much afflicted with this misfortune, that we cannot but be extremely sensible of the great mortification this must give you at this critical juncture, when you are every moment hazarding your life in the service of your country, and whilst the fate of Europe depends in so great a degree on your conduct and good success: But we are also as fully convinced that it is impossible for your Grace to quit the service at this time, without the utmost hazard to the whole alliance. And we must therefore conjure you by the glory you have already obtained, by the many services you have done your Queen and country, by the expectation you have justly raised in all Europe, and by all that is dear and tender to you at home, whose chief dependance is upon your success, that you would not leave this great work unfinished, but continue at the head of the army. This we look upon as the most necessary step that can be taken to prevent the dissolution of this Parliament.   Your Grace's compliance with this our earnest request would be the greatest obligation to us, and all that wish well to our country.   And you may depend upon it, that the contrary will be the greatest satisfaction to your enemies. We are, my Lord, your Grace's most humble, and obedient servants, COWPER C.; GODOLPHIN, SOMERS, NEWCASTLE, DEVON-SHIRE, ORFORD, HALLIFAX, H. BOYLE."

The removal of my Lord Sunderland, who was so nearly allied to the Duke of Marlborough, as it had an immediate effect on the funds and the public credit at home, so it gave an alarm to all the courts concerned in the grand alliance; an event, which brought the Queen's private counsellors under a fresh necessity of deceiving her, and engaged her to promise what they had determined she should not perform. For not only the strongest assurances were given here, that there was no thought of any other changes, but Mr. Secretary Boyle had orders from the Queen to write to the foreign courts in her name, and assure them, that all fears were groundless, and that she would continue the administration of her affairs in the hands of her present ministry, of whose abilities she had had so long experience. And yet in less than two months after this, and even the very day after the Queen had expressed her desire to my Lord Godolphin himself, that he would continue in her service, she dismissed him; and her letter of order to him to break his staff, was sent by no worthier a messenger than a man in livery, to be left with his Lordship's porter. A proceeding which in all its parts would remain very unaccountable, if the Queen herself had not, to those who expostulated with her, made this undoubtedly true declaration, *that she was sorry for it, but could not help it.* Unhappy necessity! that urged her to dismiss a minister of my Lord Godolphin's experienced abilities and integrity, and to put into his place a person, whom I indeed should be at a loss to describe, but of whom a friend of mine, many years ago, drew the following just character.

"He was a cunning and a dark man, of too small abilities to do much good, but of all the qualities requisite to do mischief, and to bring on the ruin and destruction of a nation. This mischievous darkness of his Soul was written in his countenance, and plainly legible in a very odd look, disagreeable to every body at first sight, which being joined with a constant, aukward motion or rather agitation of his head and body, betrayed a turbulent dishonesty within, even in the midst of all those familiar airs, jocular bowing and smiling, which he always affected, to cover what could not be covered. He had long accustomed himself so much to dissemble his real intentions, and to use an ambiguous and obscure way of speaking, that he could hardly ever be understood when he designed it, or be believed, when he never so much desired it. His natural temper led him to so expensive and profuse a way of living, that he had brought himself into great necessities, though he had long enjoyed the advantages of very great and profitable posts. One principal and very expensive piece of his art, in which he seems to have excelled all that went before him, was, to have in pay a great number of spies of all sorts, to let him into what was passing in all considerable families. It was remarkable, that when he came most into favour with the Queen, he was perhaps the only man, in whose ruin the two contending parties would have united, as one in whom there was no foundation to repose any confidence. And that when he came to have the greatest power with the Queen, he had lost all credit every where else."

The same necessity which forced her Majesty to dismiss my Lord Godolphin from her service, rendered her irreconcileable to me, though by means of one person at court, who happened to be in good favour with her, I made all possible attempts to remove her unjust prejudices against me. I wrote to him long and plain accounts of what had past, justifying myself, and exposing the ingratitude as well as malice of my enemies; All which accounts he read to the Queen, but without any effect upon her. She said not a word to any of these representations, except one, wherein I had set forth a faithfulness and frugality, with which I had served her in my offices; and had complained of the attempts made by the agents of her new friends to vilify me, all over the nation, as one who had cheated my mistress of vast sums of money. Her Majesty, on this occasion, was pleased to say, *every body knows, cheating is not the Duchess of Marlborough's crime,*

The same person, to try the Queen further, mentioned my coming to court, as what might be proper, on account of some *new clothes,* which, as groom of the stole, I had by her Majesty's order bought for her. But she presently charged him to advise me, as from himself, not to come. And when after a very successful campaign, the Duke of Marlborough was returned to London, the Queen most readily accepted the resignation, which he carried her from me, of my offices. The Duchess of Somerset was made groom of the stole, and had the robes; and Mrs. Masham had the privy-purse.

The Duke of Marlborough, notwithstanding an infinite variety of mortifications, by which it was endeavoured to make him resign his commission, (that there might be a pretence to raise an out-cry against him, as having quitted his Queen's and his country's service, merely because he could not govern in the cabinet, as well as in the field) continued to serve yet another campaign. All his friends here (moved by a true concern for the public) pressed him to it, the confederates called him with the utmost importunity, and Prince Eugene intreated him to come with all the earnestness and passion that could be expressed. He went; but his authority was now diminished, and his forces weakened, many of his best regiments being drawn off, some to go moulder in Spain, and others to be sacrificed in the wild expedition to Quebec. On the other hand the French had regained a spirit by the proceedings of their friends here; and they seemed to think themselves secure now of bringing disgrace upon a general, who had so often humbled *them,* and whose very name had been among them for many years a sound of terror. His masterly conduct, and his surprising success, disappointed the hope, both of our foreign and domestic enemies. The latter seemed to repent that they had permitted him to make this campaign, the happy event of which must unavoidably render a peace with France, upon French conditions, the more infamous. Yet a peace was so necessary to the preservation of the new ministers' power, that it must be had at any rate. And in order to it, the confidence of the French King must be gained. This confidence could never be hoped for, so long as the Duke of Marlborough was at the head of the army. And therefore, as all the arts of malice and detraction had proved ineffectual to make him resign his post, it was become necessary to remove him from it. But what plausible pretence to remove so able and so successful a general, while the war was, in appearance, still subsisting? A frivolous and groundless complaint in parliament about certain perquisites he had claimed, as belonging to his state, must serve the turn. The Queen, indeed, when he had laid before her what was doing him by the *commissioners of accounts,* was pleased to say, *she was sure her servants* (her new ministers) *would not encourage such proceedings.* Nevertheless, in a very short time, her Majesty, once more pressed by an irresistible necessity, made use of that very complaint as a reason for dismissing him from all his employments.

To the Queen's letter, importing this dismission, the Duke returned the following answer.

"MADAM,—I am very sensible of the honour your Majesty does me in dismissing me from your service by a letter of your own hand, though I find by it that my enemies have been able to prevail with your Majesty to do it in the manner that is most injurious to me. And if their malice and inveteracy against me had not been more powerful with them than the consideration of your Majesty's honour and justice, they would not have influenced you to impute the occasion of my dismission to a false and malicious insinuation contrived by themselves, and made public, when there was no opportunity for me to give in my answer; which they must needs be conscious would fully detect the falshood and malice of their aspersions, and not leave them that handle for bringing your Majesty to such extremities against me.

"But I am much more concerned at an expression in your Majesty's letter which seems to complain of the treatment you had met with. I know not how to understand that word, nor what construction to make of it. I know I have always endeavoured to serve your Majesty fatihfully and zealously, through a great many undeserved mortifications. But if your Majesty does intend by that expression to find fault with my not coming to the cabinet-council, I am very free to acknowledge that my duty to your Majesty and country would not give me leave to join in the counsel of a man, who, in my opinion, puts your Majesty upon all manner of extremities. And it is not my opinion only, but the opinion of all makind *that the friendship of France must needs be destructive to your Majesty : there being in that court a root of enmity irreconcileable to your Majesty's government, and the religion of these kingdoms.* I wish your Majesty may never find the want of so faithful a servant, as I have always endeavoured to approve myself to you. I am with the greatest duty and submission,   " Madam, Your Majesty's most dutiful and obedient subject,

" MARLBOROUGH."

§ III.—THUS, my Lord, I have given you a short history of my favour with my Royal Mistress, from its earliest rise to its irrecoverable fall. You have seen with admiration how *sincere* and how *great* an affection a *Queen* was capable of having for a *servant who never flattered her* And I doubt not but your friendship made some conclusions to *my* advantage, when you observed for how many years I was able to hold my place in her regard, notwithstanding her most real and invariable passion for that phantom which she called *the church :* That *darling phantom* which the tories were for ever presenting to her imagination, and employed as a *Will in the whisp,* to bewilder her mind, and entice her, (as she at last unhappily experienced) to the destruction of her quiet and her glory. But I believe you have thought that the most extraordinary thing in the whole fortune of my favour, was its being at last destroyed by a cause in appearance so unequal to the effect, I mean Mrs. Abigail Hill. For I will venture to affirm, that whatever may have been laid to my charge of ill behaviour to my Mistress in the latter years of my service, is all reducible to this one crime, *my inveteracy to poor Masham.* I have indeed said, that my constant combating the Queen's inclination to the tories did, in the end, prove the ruin of my credit with her; and this is true, in as much as without that, her Majesty could never been engaged to listen to any insinuations against me. Her passion for the church furnished the sole means by which Mrs. Masham (the machine in the hands of Harley) could take hold of her mind, and bring her by degrees, to look upon that behaviour in me, as rudeness and disrespect, which before had been only sincerity and frankness, and a warmth of zeal for her service. And yet (as you have seen) in that very letter where her Majesty tells me, *I have lost her kindness irrecoverably* she declares, *that this change is not owing to any fault I have committed.* But though the Queen, in her highest discontent with me, and after I had been in her service seven and twenty years, had no crime to lay to my charge, except *my malice to poor Masham*, yet the ready invention of others, who knew nothing of my conduct, but whose interest it was to decry me, could presently find in it abundant matter for accusation.

The calumnies against me were so gross, and yet so greedily devoured by the credulity of party rage, that I determined to write and publish something in my own justification; the following is the substance of a sort of memorial, which for that purpose I drew up in 1712. I have already related by what means I was then dissuaded from making it public, and the reasons that now induce me to pursue that design.

It was spread about in libels, that I had behaved myself unworthily in my offices, and had been unfaithful to the trusts reposed in me; that I had abused my favour with the Queen, by obtaining unreasonable and exorbitant grants to myself; and that, through an insatiable greediness of riches, I had prostituted to sale titles of honour and places of trust.

As to my conduct with respect to the Robes, this one observation is almost sufficient, that all my accounts of the robes, for the whole nine years in which I served the Queen in that office, were passed in the Exchequer with the greatest regularity; and that, in passing them, I produced acquittances for every sum to the value of twenty shillings paid to any tradesman; which was such a method of exactness as had never before been used by any master or mistress of the robes.

Upon my bringing in the first accounts of this sort, in order to have them passed, it was said, in a report made to the Treasury from Auditor Harley's office, that no such accounts had ever been brought there before. Mr. Taylor, in the Treasury, and all the clerks of that board, made the like observation. But it is most worthy to be remembered, Mr. Harley, the same Mr. Harley who was afterwards Lord Treasurer, and who then hired his creatures to misrepresent me, throughout all the nation, as no better than a pickpocket, he, I say, upon occasion of his brother's having made an extract from the accounts of former reigns of the yearly expences of the robes, wrote me the following.

" *Thursday, August 8th,* 1706.—Madam, I missed the opportunity of paying my duty to your Grace last time at Windsor, which occasions you the trouble of this letter. My brother, having made a state of your Grace's accounts, desired that I would receive your pleasure, when you would permit him to wait upon your Grace with it. *I perceive your Grace's conduct will shine on all occasions;* for my brother tells me, he has made a collection of all the accounts which have been brought in for robes for 46 years, since the year 1660, and by that it will appear, upon the comparison, how much better (to a great value) your Grace has managed for the crown. He will have the honour to present this to your Grace whenever you please to appoint a time to receive it." &c.

The yearly expence of the robes in all the reigns before Q. Anne was one year with another above 5040*l.*, and the expence of the four first years of her reign was not 2900*l.* But because there is a great difference between the expences for the robes of a queen and those of a king, it will be more equitable to compare my accounts for the robes of Queen Anne with those for Queen Mary, when under the management of Lady Derby, of which, for two years, I procured a copy from the office. It appears that in the first of those two years, the expence of Queen Mary's robes was greater by a thousand pounds than that of

Queen Anne for the whole four years mentioned in auditor Harley's collection. For the expence of those four years was no more than 11,565*l*. 7*s*. 1*d*.; the expence of the first year only of Queen Mary was 12,604*l*. 12*s*. 2*d*. In the second year the expence of Queen Mary's robes was 11,131*l*. 9*s*. 1*d*., being little short of the whole expence of the said four years of Queen Anne.

After these four years, the expence of the following five years (which make up the whole amount of my service) amounting to 18,972*l*. 9*s*. 10*d*. was more in proportion than that of the said four preceding years. This was chiefly occasioned by the extraordinary expence on account of the mourning for the Prince, and the Queen's ordering every thing belonging to the robes of what kind soever to be given away, so that at the end of the mourning all were new at once, and amongst them some very rich clothes, which happened just before I left the office. These two articles necessarily made a considerable increase of the ordinary expence, especially as the Queen gave 600*l*. to the maids of honour to buy them mourning. However, the yearly expence of my nine years, taken one with another, is very small in comparison with the two years before-mentioned, when Lady Derby managed Queen Mary's robes. For the sum total paid by the Exchequer on account of the robes in my nine years amounts only to 32,050*l*. 1*s*. 3*d*, from which deduct the coronation expence, 1512*l*. 4*s*. 4*d*., and there will remain 30,537*l*. 16*s*. 11*d*. being 3393*l*. 1*s*. 9*d*. 1*q*. for the yearly expence during the said nine years. In this sum are included the salaries and other matters belonging to the robes, being about 1400*l*. p. an. which I always put into my account (because I thought it the fairest way), but which before my time were put into a separate account, that the account of the robes might appear the less. Subtract this 1400*l*. from the 3393*l*. 1*s*. 9*d*. 1*q*. the remainder (the yearly expence of Queen Anne's robes in my nine years) is only 1993*l*. 1*s* 9*d*. 1*q*. which is less than the yearly expence of Queen Mary's robes, according to Lady Derby's account, by the yearly sum of 9874*l*. 18*s*. 10*d*. 1*q*. So that it evidently appears that by my economy in the nine years I served her Majesty, I saved her near 90,000*l*.

To show, however, how much people were determined to defame me at any rate, and at all adventures, I had the fortune, that while some accused me of being *too profuse* of the Queen's money, others censured me as being *too saving* of it, and too hard upon the tradesmen I dealt with. I will therefore give some account of these matters.

It is very well known, that in the preceding reigns, the tradesmen gave money to serve the crown, which brought in great sums to the masters of the robes, but at the same time obliged the tradesmen to charge extravagant prices for their goods, a privilege which could hardly be disputed with them, considering the sums they had given for the custom, and the accidents they were then always exposed to by the death of the Prince, or the death or removal of the master of the robes. But the tradesmen whom I made use of had nothing of this to plead; they gave no money to serve the crown, nor were put to any expence, not so much as the customary one of poundage; they were paid regularly, ran no manner of hazard, and had no more trouble in serving the Queen than in serving a common customer, and therefore I did not think it reasonable that they should be allowed above a shilling or two in the pound extraordinary for their goods. But those who had the honour to *see* the Queen, and to make her clothes, were allowed more than the double of what they had from the first quality. And this was all I thought myself at liberty to do in an office in which I was entirely trusted.

My method to prevent all mistakes or abuses, was always to sign the tradesmens' bills at the same that they delivered their goods. They were paid by Mrs. Thomas, a person of whose honesty I had had long experience, and to whom I had given the employment of chief of the robes, making it worth to her between two and three hundred pounds a year, not by a salary, but by old clothes and other little advantages; and I had a promise from her, never to take money of any of the tradesmen. It is very certain that she was punctual to this promise, and if any of the tradesmen themselves are still living, they will I am sure bear witness to it.

I now come to my management of the privy-purse, the yearly allowance for which was 20,000l. not half the sum allowed in King William's time, and indeed very little, considering how great a charge there was fixed upon it by custom, the Queen's bounties, healing gold, and charities, besides the many pensions that were paid out of it. The allowance was augmented to 26,000l. two years before I left the office. But in those two years Mrs. Masham was become the great dispenser of the Queen's money, I only bringing to her Majesty the sums that were called for.

The privy-purse is not subject to any account by law, notwithstanding which I observed the same method with regard to this as with regard to the robes, taking acquittances from all persons to whom I paid any money, and *from the Queen herself for all sums paid into her own hands*, as likewise a discharge from her Majesty upon every account given in, which discharge was in these words, " I have examined these accounts, and am satisfied they are right. ANNE R." The money of the privy-purse was paid upon my notes, by Mr. Goggs, a goldsmith over-against St. Clement's church, whom I strictly charged never to take any poundage, which used constantly to be taken before my time. But I thought it would be as mean as it was inhuman, to deduct from charities, and make advantage of the indigence of others, and therefore I broke that custom. Let any one then judge from the whole, whether I did not put this office into such a method, as rendered it impossible for me to cheat the Queen, even supposing I could at any time have been base enough to desire it.

The second charge against me is, that of abusing my favour with the Queen, by obtaining unreasonable and exorbitant grants to myself.

I have never been disposed to deny any of the Queen's favours to me; I have always remembered them with gratitude, and freely spoke of them as there was occasion; and I shall here give a particular account of all the grants and bounties I ever had from her.

I have in the former part of this relation, taken notice of my being appointed one of the ladies of her bed-chamber, at her own request, upon her marriage with the Prince of Denmark. The salary of this place was 200l. a year,

I have mentioned also that her Royal Highness, upon the Countess of Clarendon's leaving her to go to Ireland, advanced me to be first Lady of the bed-chamber; by which promotion I came to have a yearly salary of 400l.

I have further related, that the Princess soon after her obtaining a settlement by Parliament of 50,000l. a year, believing, that she owed the ease and independency of her condition to the zeal, industry, and diligence of my Lord

---

* The principal of them were Mr. Vernon, Mr. Inchly, Mr. Sands upon Ludgate-hill, and Mr. Alexander in Covent-garden, all mercers. Mrs. Devent, Mrs. Tombes and Mr. Bagshaw, who kept Indian shops, and Mr. Eliot (since succeded by his nephew) a lace-man in the Strand.

Marlborough and myself upon that occasion, was pleased to grant me, of her own motion, an annual pension of 1000l. And I cannot here entirely pass over the intention, which her Royal Highness had of giving us another mark of her favour, when my Lord Marlbourough fell into disgrace with King William. She would have made a new office for him in her court, like that which Lord Berkeley had in her father's. But as soon as I was apprized of this design, I dissuaded her from it; because I thought it not reasonable on her own account; and besides, as I lived in friendship with Sir Benjamin Bathurst, who would have been hurt by the creation of such an office, I thought this a sufficient reason for declining the offer.

A little before the Princess came to the crown, my eldest daughter was to be married to Lord Godolphin's son, on which occasion her Highness wrote to me in these terms.

"I have a request to make to my dear Mrs. Freeman. It is, that whenever dear Lady Hariotte marries, you would give me leave to give her something to keep me in her thoughts—and concluded thus,—I beg my poor mite may be accepted, being offered from a heart that is without any reserve with more passion and sincerity my dear Mrs. Freeman's, than any other can be capable of."

The mite which the Princess here speaks of was 10,000l. the whole portion that was to be paid on my daughter's marriage. It had always been the custom for the crown to give portions to the daughters of their favourites, but the Princess having but 50,000l. a year, I thought the offer too large for her income, and would therefore accept no more than the half of it.

The like sum of 5000l. the Princess gave to my second daughter when she was married to Lord Sunderland, adding a promise at the same time to take care of all my children.

I fancy, my Lord, if you consider only the almost unparalleled affection the Queen had for me, you will be little surprised, either at these expressions of it, or those which I am going to relate. And you will certainly be much less so, if you can believe the Queen herself in a matter, where perhaps it would not become me to expatiate, I mean the proofs I had given her of my affectionate fidelity in her service, and inviolable attachment to her interests and happiness. It would be as endless as it is needless to transcribe all the letters I have from her to this purpose. A few extracts from some of them will be sufficient.

On occasion of something done for the Prince in King William's time, she wrote to me in these terms.

"I was going to thank your Lord myself for what was done last night concerning the Prince's business, it being wholly owing to your and his kindness, or else I am sure it would never have been brought to any effect. But I durst not do it for fear of not being able to express the true sense of my poor heart, and therefore I must desire my dear Mrs. Freeman to say a great deal both for, Mr. Morley, and myself: and though we are poor in words, yet he so just as to believe we are truly sensible and most faithfully yours. And as for your faithful Morley, be assured she is more, if it be possible, than ever, her dear dear, Mrs. Freeman's."

In another, after complaining to me of being ill served (as indeed she was to a very great degree) she adds,———

"Though it will be impossible for me to have every thing done to my mind, unless I could meet with a Mrs. Freeman in every post of my family; but her fellow I do really believe is not to be found the world over, and I am sure I never can have any friend that will be so dear to me as she is."

In another——(I forget upon what occasion)——" I give you millions of thanks for all your and Mr. Freeman's kindness, which I am more truly sensible of than I can express, and shall never be satisfied with any thing I can either do or say in return; for where one owes so much, one can never get out of debt: but whilst I have life, I will endeavour to shew my dear Mrs. Freeman, I have a grateful heart that is most passionately and faithfully at her command."

When her Royal Highness was pleased to give the 5000*l.* I have mentioned on my eldest daughter's marriage, I wrote her a letter full of gratitude and respect. At that time I kept no copies of my letters, having no suspicion that I should ever have occasion for such vouchers, however the Princess's answer will show the tenour of what I wrote, as well as her Highness's sentiments in my regard.

"My dear Mrs. Freeman has no reason to be uneasy with the thoughts that she can never do enough to deserve my kindness, for she has done more than ever any mortal did to merit another's friendship. And it is very kind in setting so great a value upon so poor an expression as I have made of my truth, *which upon my word I am not satisfied with, it coming far short of what my heart is inclined to do.* But as long as I live, I must be endeavouring to shew, that never any body had a sincerer passion for another, than I have for dear Mrs. Freeman."

All these favours I received from the Princess before she came to the crown, soon after which, I had the following letter from her, which as it shews the continuance of her sincere affection for me, will at the same time serve for a voucher *that I did not accept the whole* that was offered for a portion to my eldest daughter.

" *Friday Morning.*—My Lord Bridgewater being in haste to be married, I cannot any longer defer telling my dear Mrs. Freeman, what I have intended a great while, that I hope she will now give me leave to do what I had a mind to when dear Lady Hariotte was married, and let me speak to my Lord Treasurer about it when I see him," &c.

This letter was a kind proof that the Queen had not forgot her promise of providing for all my children, which she afterwards fully performed by giving the like portion to my fourth daughther.

I shall now mention all the grants made to myself during the whole time that I served her Majesty.

The first was the office of ranger of the great and little parks at Windsor. This I esteemed as a great favour, because the lodge in the great park (the same that Mr. May enjoyed many years, and after him the Earl of Portland) is a very agreeable place to live in: and because her Majesty was pleased to give it me of her own accord, remembering that when we used in former days to ride by it, I had often wished for such a place. The lodge in the little park at that time was no better than such as the underkeepers live in, and I gave it to a brother of the Duke of Marlborough's who was so well pleased with the situation as to lay out five or six thousand pounds upon it; of which the crown will have the advantage after one life, as also of between four and five thousand pounds that I laid out upon the lodge in the great park.

This grant used to be represented to the public as worth 4000*l.* a year: but all the keepers, and many of the inhabitants of Windsor know, that I never made any advantage of it worth mentioning, unless the milk of a few cows and a little firing when I was there may be reckoned such. And how indeed can it be imagined, that any other profits could arise from it (without taking away the very allowances of the keepers) when it is remembered, that to answer the crown warrants, it is necessary to keep up four or five thousand head of deer in the park, for which the allowance was but 500l. a year (which however was taken from me some years ago) and that the ranger must be at the expence of making, and sometimes of buying hay for the deer: that the keepers wages were payable out of this allowance, with several other expences which in parks belonging to the crown are much greater than in others? So that the thing had plainly very little to recommend it, besides the pleasantness of the habitation.

The next grant, of which by my Lord Godolphin's means I obtained the promise from the Queen, after the Queen dowager's death, was the ground in St. James's Park upon which my house stands. This has been valued by my enemies at 10,000l. how justly let any one determine, who will consider that a certain rent is paid for it to the Exchequer, that the grant was at first but for fifty years, and that the building has cost between forty and fifty thousand pounds, of which the Queen never paid one shilling, though many people have been made to believe otherwise.

These were the only grants I ever had from the Queen except one, which occasioned the witty comparison that was made between me and the lady's woman, who out of her mistress's pin-money of 26l. put twenty-two into her own pocket. The matter was this. At the Queen's accession to the government, she used to lament to me, that the crown being impoverished by former grants, she wanted the power her predecessors had enjoyed to reward faithful servants; and she desired me to take out of the privy-purse 2000l. a year, in order to some purchase for my advantage. I made my grateful acknowledgments to her Majesty, but as she had provided for my children, and as the offices I enjoyed by her favour brought me in more than I wanted, I could not think it reasonable to accept her offer; and I absolutely refused it. The Queen some time after, in two several letters, pressed me to receive this bounty, and she frequently did the same by word of mouth. Nevertheless I constantly declined it; until the time, that, notwithstanding the uncommon regard I had shown to her Majesty's interest and honour in the execution of my trusts, she was pleased to dismiss me from her service. Then indeed it was thought I had no longer the same reason to be scrupulous on this head. By the advice of my friends, I sent the Queen one of her own letters, in which she had pressed me to take the 2000l. a year; and I wrote at the same time to ask her Majesty, whether she would allow me to charge in the privy-purse accounts, which I was to send her, that yearly sum from the time of the offer, amounting to 18,000l. Her Majesty was pleased to answer, that I might charge it. This therefore I did, *inserting in my accounts* (which were a kind of *memorial*) these words:

" After the Princess came to the crown, she was pleased to write to me to take 2000l. a year out of the privy-purse, and *to make no more words of it*, and lay it up to do something with it; because, she added, she had not power to do as others had done before her, to reward faithful services. And I might own or conceal it as I liked best; for she did not care who knew what she gave to one she could never reward enough."

Her Majesty after keeping my accounts a sufficient time to have them carefully examined, (I suppose by Mr. Harley) returned them to me signed in this manner.

"*Feb.* ⅴ, 17✝✝.—I have examined these Accounts, and allow of them.

"ANNE R."

If some persons may be inclined to censure my conduct in this particular as too interested, yet every body must, I think, be candid enough to own, that it shewed a consciousness of my integrity in the discharge of my trusts, and that I feared no accusation upon that head, even from malice in power. Nay I will venture to say, that impartial judges will not think this part of my behaviour liable to any criticism, when they remember and consider, that by my unprecedented fidelity and economy in the discharge of my offices, I saved to her Majesty not only more than the sum in question, but more than the whole value of all the gratuities I ever had from her. For besides the bounties I have already mentioned, the Queen after her coming to the crown, never made me the present of a diamond, or of any thing worth taking notice of during the whole time that I was in her favour.

As to my offices under the Queen they were indeed considerable, and I have ever acknowledged them to be so, amounting to 5600*l.* a year, deducting only for taxes and fees. But it is to be remembered, that they were only the same employments that I had executed when she was Princess at the salary of 400*l.* a year; and it was therefore nothing extraordinary that she should continue me in them when she came to be Queen. And in what manner I discharged these offices, I have already related.

I come now to the third article of accusation against me, *That I prostituted to sale titles of honour and places of trust.*

As for *titles of honour,* I never was concerned in making any peer but one, and that was my Lord Hervey the present Earl of Bristol. I had made a promise to Sir Thomas Felton, when the Queen came first to the crown, that if her Majesty should ever make any new Lords, I would certainly use my interest that Mr. Hervey might be one. And accordingly, though I was retired into the country under the most sensible affliction for the death of my only son, yet when the Queen had resolved to create four peers, Granville, Guernsey, Gower and Conway, I had such a regard to my word, that I wrote to Lord Marlborough and Lord Godolphin, that if they did not endeavour to get Mr. Hervey made a peer, I neither would nor could shew my face any more. The thing was done purely at my request, and at a time when affairs at court ran so violently against the whole party of whigs, that Mr. Hervey had laid aside all hopes of the peerage, and was therefore surprised to the last degree, when a message came to him from the Duke of Marlborough, that he must come on such a day by the backstairs, to kiss the Queen's hand for being made a peer. On this occasion my Lady Hervey wrote to me in the following terms.

"*March* 14, 1702.—MADAM.—Mr. Hervey and myself have both so long and justly sacrificed the satisfaction of our own, to the ease and quiet of your Grace's mind, that could you know what incessant importunities we have resisted from the one, you would the easier forgive the unseasonable interruptions we fear this must at last prove to the other; but the sense of our obligations to your Grace calls too clamorously upon us to be any farther withstood, and therefore we rather venture this intrusion upon your solitude, than to be longer silent upon a subject, which requires the earliest endeavours after all returns that can be made your Grace by us for it. I know nothing we have so much at heart (unless it be the due sympathy we feel of your Grace's present condition) as how we may in some sort deserve the great honour her Majesty has been so graciously pleased to bestow on us and our family, by your Grace's kind mediation, and how we may ever acquit ourselves of so generous a piece of friendship towards your Grace, which I am very sure we both think the future study of our lives can never enough compensate, unless your Grace's usual goodness will accept of the most zealous and grateful wills for payment, and then we conclude the chief of those very many, whom you have bound to be your Grace's well wishers must remain, as much if not more indebted to you than I know Mr. Hervey (so qualified) to be as well as.

"Madam, Your Grace's most obliged, and faithful humble servant,

"E. HERVEY."

This letter would alone be a sufficient proof, that the service I then did was not the purchase of money; but my Lord Bristol is still living, who will vouch for the truth of this account.

Certain it is, that I might have made considerable profit by this sort of traffic, could I have thought it consistent with justice and honour. I was offered 6000l. to get Mr. Coke of Norfolk made a peer. And how easy and inoffensive a thing would this have been at that time? For he was a gentleman of an estate equal to the title desired, and was grandson to the Duke of Leeds, and in that interest which then carried all before it at court. The answer I gave to the proposal was to this effect:

That I thought her Majesty, the fountain of honour, should never bestow it but upon true merit, and as an encouragement to such persons as were considerable enough to be useful to their Prince; and that the granting the peerage upon such generous conditions, was the most likely way to oblige those she honoured with it, and strongly engage them to her service; to which they would look upon themselves as but little bound on account of their titles, if these were the purchase of their own money.

And as I was never carried by avarice to concern myself in procuring titles of honour for others, so I shall take occasion to observe here, that ambition had no share in procuring that new title, which, by her Majesty's favour to my Lord Marlborough, I myself acquired. The following letters will be some proof of it. The first is from my Lord Godolphin.

Tuesday Night, Oct. 22.—"By the enclosed address from the House of Lords, which is to be presented to the Queen to-morrow, you will see they take notice very thankfully of the benefits they receive from her Majesty's protection, and mention her good successes with better grace for her, in my opinion, than if she had done it herself.

"I shall send a copy of this address to-morrow by the post to my Lord Marlborough, because I believe it will be a satisfaction to him. I am apt to think Mrs. Morley may say something to you upon this subject, which perhaps you may not like; but I think it must be endured upon such an occasion, when it is visible to all the world, that it is not done upon your own account."——

My Lord had rightly conjectured; for I received a letter of the same date with his, from the Queen, upon the same subject.

St. James's, Thursday 22 Oct.—"I have had this evening the satisfaction of my dear Mrs. Freeman's of yesterday, for which I give you many thanks, and though I think it a long time since I saw you, I do not desire you to come one minute sooner to town than it is easy to you, but will wait with patience for the happy hour, and only beg when you do come you would send for a coach, and not make use of a chaise. Lord Treasurer intends to send you a copy of the address from the House of Lords, which is to be given me to-morrow, and that gives me an opportunity of mentioning a thing to you, that I did not intend to do yet. It is very uneasy to your poor, unfortunate, faithful Morley to think she has so very little in her power to show how truly sensible I am of all my Lord Marlborough's kindness, especially at a time when he deserves all that a rich crown could give. But since there is nothing else at this time, I hope you will give me leave, as soon as he comes, to make him a Duke. I know my dear Mrs. Freeman does not care for any thing of that kind, nor I am not satisfied with it, because it does not enough express the value I have for Mr. Freeman, nor nothing ever can how passionately I am yours, my dear Mrs. Freeman."

The other letter from my Lord Godolphin, as far as it relates to this affair, is in these terms.

" *Saturday night.*—I give you many thanks for the favour of your letter, which I received this evening. I did easily believe Mrs. Morley's letter would make you uneasy, but having her commands not to speak of it, I durst not say any more, than just to prepare you to submit to what I found by her she was convinced was necessary for the satisfaction of the public. I have waited upon her this evening to let her see how truly uneasy you were, and have begged of her, when she sees you, not to part till she has made you easy again, either by your submitting to please her, or by her condescending to cure your apprehensions."

As these letters from my Lord Godolphin were written at a time when there could not be even the remotest view of making them public, they shew that in his opinion, at least, I was not ambitious of a higher title, which indeed I considered as what would serve only to provoke malice, without giving me the least degree of pleasure.

As to *selling Places,* which was the last thing I was to clear myself from, I shall now give an account of my conduct with respect to this charge, from the time that I came first into any office at court.

A little before I succeeded Lady Clarendon in the post of first lady of the bedchamber to the Princess of Denmark, her Highness wrote to me, that she intended to take two new pages of the back-stairs, but that she would not do it till my Lady Clarendon was gone, that I might have the advantage of putting them in, meaning, that I might have the advantage of selling those two places. For it must be remarked, that at that time no person who was in any office at court, with places in his disposal, made any more scruple of selling them, than of receiving his settled salary, or the rents of his estate. It is no great wonder, therefore, that being a young courtier, and not very rich, and having such an express direction from my mistress, I followed the prevailing custom, and sold those two places. Yet it was not long before I began to condemn in my own mind this practice. There was something I thought that felt wrong in the selling of employments, and from this thought I came presently to a resolution, never more to make any advantage to myself by such means. And when, some time after, the Princess thought proper to part with her Roman catholic servants, three in number, of whom two were pages of the back-stairs, and of which two one had bought his place of me at the time before mentioned, and paid 400*l.* for it, I gave him back the whole sum; and I gave the like sum to the other Roman catholic page, though he had risen to this employment from being footman, and without money. Nay, I procured for this man, (whose name was Guyn) the continuation of his salary for life, which I mention, only that I may speak of his uncommon gratitude: For during five and twenty years afterwards, I did not set out upon a journey from London, without finding him at my coach side full of his good wishes for my health and happiness.

The first vacancy that happened under the Prince (whose confidence in me was equal to that of the Princess) was of the place of groom of the bedchamber. This I procured for Mr. Maul, who knowing what was usual in such cases, sent a message to me, desiring leave to make me a present, to which I immediately returned answer, that I was resolved against every thing of that kind

Another place that became vacant under the Prince was that of groom of the stole, which being given to my Lord Delawar, he brought a present of 500*l*. to Mr. Guidot, for me; but Mr. Guidot, who knew my dislike of such Practices, quickly satisfied him that I would not accept of it. I had afterwards many letters from his Lordship, and some but a little before my leaving the court, full of the greatest acknowledgments; and to him I always appealed for the truth of this fact.

I also refused a present from my Lord Lexington, who employed Mr. Scarborough, to make me the offer, when his Lordship was desirous to be master of the horse to the Prince.

When the Queen came to the crown, I had every day much greater opportunities than before, of making advantage of her favour, but I invariably adhered to the resolution I had taken : And I doubt not but every candid person will be perfectly convinced of this, when I have finished what I have to say upon the subject.

Had I been disposed to heap up money by the sale of employments, I should certainly not have neglected to sell those, which by virtue of my offices were in my own disposal. I might have done it with the greatest ease ; and custom had given me a sort of right to do it : But I could never think of selling my own favour, any more than that of my royal mistress,

The first places, which I had to dispose of, were those of the three pages of the backstairs; places so considerable, that several grooms of the stole were credibly said to have sold them for a thousand guineas each. But these I gave freely to Mr. Kirk, Mr. Saxton, and Mr. Smith, and purely at the request of three Ladies, the Lady Charlotte Beverwaert, the Lady Fitzharding, and the Countess of Plymouth.

The other places in my disposal were in the office of the robes—waiters, coffer-bearers, groom of the wardrobe, chief of the robes, starcher, sempstress.

Were the persons I have named above, and those to whom I gave these last mentioned employments, all, or most of them now living, as they were in 1712, when this account was first drawn up, their testimony (to which I had there appealed) would have amounted to a *positive* proof of my integrity and disinterestedness on these occasions. But as this kind of proof cannot now be had, so neither is it wanted, there being still a *negative one*, which, I am persuaded, must appear no less strong and irresistible. And it is this.

My enemies at a time, when they had all power in their hands, when they had raised such a spirit of virulence and malice as would make any thing to my prejudice readily believed, when they both could and would have amply rewarded any person, that was capable of proving the base practices they charged me with, even *then* I say, all their accusations were general; they were never able to fix upon me any one particular action, either unjust, mercenary, or even ungenerous in the use I made of my royal mistress's favour, or in the management of my own great offices. Nay, they never pretended to name or to appeal to any one person for a proof of what they laid to my charge.

But my Lord, all I have hitherto said on this article of accusation, is to satisfy those, who are not acquainted with me. Those who are, will, I am persuaded, believe me, upon my *word*, when I affirm, as I here solemnly do, that (excepting the pages' money above-mentioned) I never received the value of one shilling in money or jewels, or in any other form, either directly or indirectly, by myself, or by any other person, for procuring any place or preferment, or any title of honour, or any employment in my own disposal, or, in a word, for doing any favour during my whole life.

20th Jan. 1742.   I am, MY LORD, &c.

Printed by and for J. Davis,
14, *Charlotte-Street, Bloomsbury.*

Breinigsville, PA USA
21 November 2010
249766BV00004B/42/P